DENNIS HOPPER

MOVIE TOP TEN

CREATION

DENNIS HOPPER: MOVIE TOP TEN
Edited by Jack Hunter
ISBN 1 871592 86 0
A Butcherbest Production
© Creation Books & individual contributors 1999
Creation Movie Top Tens: a periodical, review-based publication
First published 1999 by:
Creation Books International
Design/layout/typesetting:
Bradley Davis, PCP International
Cover illustration:
"Blue Velvet"

Photo credits:
All photos by courtesy of the BFI, London; Museum Of Modern Art, New York; and the Jack Hunter Collection.

British Library Cataloguing in Publication Data:
A catalogue record for this book is available from the British Library

Editor's acknowledgements
Thanks to: All the contributors, in particular Jack Sargeant, Mikita Brottman and Chris Campion.

Creation Books
"Popular books for popular people"

CONTENTS

INTRODUCTION
"WORKING WITH THE ACCIDENT"

"I was an Abstract Expressionist before I knew there was such a thing," Dennis Hopper once said[1]. And his acting style certainly has parallels with the modernist art of Pollock, DeKooning and Rauschenberg; art that relied more on instinct than learned technique, concerned with the outward, oft-times brutal, expression of movement, fragmentation and chaos. Spanning five decades, and over a hundred feature appearances, Dennis Hopper has created his own bizarre cinema of madness and excess; a freak show that blurs fact with fiction, merging real and imagined personas. At times the events of his life have been too unbelievable for any movie. If this gritty survivor had done even half the things that have been written about him (or that he has claimed for himself) he wouldn't be here today. But he is, and even more amazingly, these days Hopper looks a pillar of health as he flits across screens. Now as an icon of a long-lost counter cultural age, he appears in, of all things, a self-referential car advertisement. The familiar close-cropped platinum hair and maniacal grin gleam into the rear-view mirror of his shiny, new vehicle at his bygone hippie self cruising the highways in **Easy Rider**.

Born in Dodge City, Kansas in 1936, Hopper grew up on a farm with his maternal grandparents. As a boy he picked up Gene Fowler's *Minutes Of The Last Meeting*, a precursor to Kenneth Anger's *Hollywood Babylon* that detailed the boozy lives of actors like W.C. Fields and John Barrymore. Hopper says he came away with the impression that an artist was "a drinker-drugger"[2], and spent the next forty-odd years of his life trying to live up to it. By then, he was already experimenting with altered states of mind by sniffing gasoline out of the tank of his grandfather's truck. "I got to see fantastic things," he recalled. "One day, I went crazy from it, took a baseball bat, and broke everything on the truck."[3]

Arriving in Hollywood in 1954, aged 18, with dreams of becoming the next Orson Welles or John Barrymore, Hopper's first stage work was a walk-on part in *The Postman Rings Twice*. With a letter of recommendation from his job as a gofer for David O. Selznick's LaJolla Playhouse, he secured a Hollywood agent, a Screen Actor's Guild card and a role as an epileptic in the TV series, *Medic*. Watching Brando and Clift emote on screen in **Viva Zapata!** and **Place In The Sun** changed all Hopper's notions of acting, but it was James Dean that provided the persona he was to adopt. Ironically, his first big break was shadowing Dean as "Goon" in **Rebel Without A Cause** (a partnership also repeated in **Giant**).

With Dean's death, Hopper determined to inherit his legacy as a bad boy actor who lived life to the limits. It was noted that soon after he started behaving somewhat eccentrically, but all he achieved was getting blacklisted from every major studio. Hopper claims it was due to his refusal to take direction from Henry Hathaway while making 1958's **From Hell To Texas**. Others cite his general attitude at a time when the studios were cutting back on contract actors; Hopper simply wasn't a major enough talent to merit special treatment.

The starring role in Curtis Harrington's bizarre **Night Tide**, playing a sailor who falls for a mermaid in a freak show, was Hopper's first cinematic connection to Hollywood counter-culture. But there was little other work for him in L.A., save a few stock roles in Westerns or B-movies such as **Key Witness**, so he upped and moved to New York, where he studied acting and found work as a portrait and fashion photographer for *Vogue* and *Harpers Bazaar*.

Hopper became a "gallery bum" and was eventually given a job by Irving Blonde who ran the Ferris, Paris Gallery, shooting portraits of artists whose work was exhibited there, among them Warhol and Lichtenstein. (He continues to be a passionate collector of modern art; his mentor in this pursuit was none other than Vincent Price. Acquisitions include work by Warhol, Rauschenberg, Johns, Basquiat – Hopper played art dealer Bruno Bischofberger in Julian Schnabel's 1996 biopic of the artist).

Progressing to what he calls his Cartier Bresson period, he framed shots of the city and waited on sidewalks for something to happen. He also shot iconic portraits of celebrity friends, bikers and Civil Rights marches. (A book of his photographs, *Out Of The Sixties*, was published in the '80s.) But, he considered photographs just a practice run – "I didn't crop my photographs, I was learning to work within the frame of movies."[4]

Back in L.A., in between the drink, the drugs, and the sex (Hopper: "I had so much pussy in the '60s my beard was like a glazed donut"), there were marriages (one, to Michelle Phillips of the Mamas And Papas, lasting some three days) and, sporadically, films; roles in "counter-culture" exploitationers like Corman's **The Trip** and the Monkees vehicle **Head** all led Hopper nearer to his eventual goal: to direct films. This, after all, was the ultimate autocratic role for a man whose actions were solely determined by self (as Peter Fonda, his collaborator on **Easy Rider**, was to find out).

A family friend of Hopper's first wife, Brooke Hayward (daughter of actress Margaret Sullivan and agent Leland Hayward), Peter Fonda had befriended Hopper while both were making B-movies biker flicks for Roger Corman. Together, they hatched a plan to make their own biker movie (but one tuned into the counter culture), and secured "Monkees money" from Bob Rafelson and Bert Schneider to make **Easy Rider**. Ever since the film's

Key Witness

release and subsequent phenomenal success – $40 million and counting from a half million dollar investment – the source of its inspiration has been a major bone of contention between a number of parties. In 1996, Hopper tried to get Fonda to sign a declaration that he alone wrote the screenplay, then sued him for withholding millions of dollars in royalties. Terry Southern, who had been brought on board to knock the script idea into shape, had already been brushed off with a one-off $5,000 payment without a look in at the enormous profits. And, writer John Gilmore claims that the story actually came from a treatment he passed to Hopper called "Out Takes", based on Gilmore's own experiences of riding with James Dean in the '50s.[5]

As the film's producer, Fonda found the nature of his collaboration with Hopper on **Easy Rider** change on the very first day of shooting at the New Orleans Mardi Gras. "This is my fucking movie, and nobody is going to take it away from me," he recalls Hopper screaming maniacally at the assembled cast and crew over and over until his voice gave out. First thing the next morning, the same thing happened. "Dennis was two-for-two in the batshit department," deadpans Fonda, "transformed into a little fascist freak

I'd only glimpsed before."[6] Still, Fonda had nothing but praise for his director's ability to capture the moment on film.

"Cocteau said something about working with the accident," Hopper once mused. "In directing, I go with the moment-to-moment-reality level; I work on the premise 'if you see it, get it'. But editing is very painful, like being in prison. Editing is like being in a prison. It's creative, but there's also something very uncreative about it. Sort of like framing a picture."[7] Tangled up in this "framing" process, Hopper spent twenty-two weeks editing **Easy Rider** and produced a four hour cut, including a "scene missing" title card that he intended to fill with fifteen minutes of Mardi Gras footage. Fonda and the producers sent him home to Taos, New Mexico for a break, while they cut the movie down to a manageable length. On seeing it, Hopper yelled that they had ruined his movie.

There was no such safety-net for **The Last Movie**, which took almost a year and a half to edit. His eagerly-awaited follow-up to **Easy Rider** was, Hopper believed, a definitive statement on the film industry and cinematic art. It was also the point where his film-making criss-crossed into modern art, with its story within a story structure and impressionistic editing style. To Hopper's delight, the completed movie won the Grand Prize at the Venice Film Festival in 1971, but then Universal Studios told him they would give it only a limited theatrical release unless it was re-edited to comply with their wishes. Hopper refused, and they buried the film, which also got critically panned.

Crushed with the failure of his grand artistic statement, Hopper retreated to Taos. His second dalliance with Hollywood was over – Hopper claims he only made one film in America during the next twelve years, Henry Jaglom's **Tracks**, in which he plays a battle-scarred soldier accompanying a dead buddy's coffin back to its final resting place. The intense disappointment he experienced over the failure of **The Last Movie** led to arguably Hopper's most interesting period; ten years in the wilderness during which his legendary excess began to haemorrhage into his performances. After a promising role in the mythic Western **Kid Blue** (1973) alongside Warren Oates, Hopper let rip as drunken poet Chicken in **The Sky Is Falling** (Silvio Narizzano, 1976); the eponymous Irish outlaw in **Mad Dog Morgan** (Philippe Mora, 1976); manic war photographer, Hurley, in **Apocalypse Now** (1979); art forger Tom Ripley in **The American Friend** (1977); and abusive father Donny Barnes in **Out Of The Blue** (1980, also his third directorial project, which proved to be one of his most coherent, powerful and involving statements).

Apart perhaps from **The Osterman Weekend** (Sam Peckinpah's last movie) and Francis Ford Coppola's experimental gang flick **Rumble Fish** (both 1983), Hopper's choice of projects around this time became increasingly

bizarre, including Bigas Lunas' **Reborn** (1981) and Roland Klick's **White Star** (1981), two particularly trashy European movies, in which he played, respectively, a born-again preacher and rock manager. The latter even contains one of the most degrading scene of Hopper's career, where he is cornered by a gang of punks in a public toilet, kicked, beaten with pool cues and pissed on. And still manages to stand up sneering.

Few actors would have exposed themselves as mercilessly as Hopper did. It's possible Hopper simply had no idea what he was doing. He claimed his primary addiction was to alcohol – half a gallon of rum a day plus beer and martini chasers – and used cocaine – several grams a day – just to keep him balanced out on set. But as his senses becoming progressively deadened, his need became greater, hastening a total loss of grip on reality. The stories of his breakdown are the stuff of legends.

At one point, Hopper heard voices talking to him over the telephone wires and believed there was a Mafia contract out on his life. So while promoting **Out Of The Blue** in Portland, Oregon, he went for broke and pulled a stunt called The Russian Suicide Death Chair (said to have been used by the Bolsheviks during the Russian Revolution to stage fake executions of nobility). An invited audience arrived at a speedway track after the film screening to find Hopper hunched underneath a chair packed with explosives. The idea being that the vacuum caused by the explosion would spare him from obliteration. To a collective baited breath, the dynamite was lit, the chair blew apart violently and Hopper emerged soon after, shaken but not stirred.

The final freak-out came when he went to make a movie called **Jungle Fever** in Mexico playing, irony of ironies, a D.E.A. agent, and became immersed in a self-induced Boschian nightmare. After checking into his hotel, coked to the eyeballs and drunk to the gills, Hopper "became convinced that there were people in the bowels of this place being tortured and being cremated." To escape the horrific visions, he went for a walk around the town, took off all his clothes (because he felt bugs crawling all over him) and got lost in the jungle, which he thought was a war zone. Come morning, the local police picked him up, still naked, and dumped him in jail, where the frantic actor thought he heard his friends being machine-gunned to death outside. When security guards from the film set came to escort him onto a plane home, Hopper imagined cameras watching his every move. As the plane taxied for take off, he saw the wing burst into flames, and took it as his chance to escape by tearing open a hatch and scaling the wing.[8]

Back in the US, Hopper admitted his drink problem, counteracted with enough cocaine to drive himself into the black, and was committed to Cedars-Sinai sanatorium. There he stayed until **Easy Rider** producer Bert Schneider had Hopper released into his care and helped him on the road to recovery. As he predicted, Hopper had broken through the limits of

Speed

experience, but was damn lucky to make it out the other side.

The crawl back from the pit of despair began in 1986, a year widely credited as the turning point in his career. He finally kicked narcotics and traded the sobriquet of "alcoholic" for "workaholic", making a total six films in one year. Without doubt, it was his portrayal of Frank Booth, the sneering, psychosexual murderer in David Lynch's **Blue Velvet** that single-handedly restored his reputation. It marked perhaps the first time Hopper had managed to channel his dark side completely into a character, rather than as a natural outpouring of his torment. Other notable appearances that year included **River's Edge** (as Feck, the oddball ex-con with a sex-doll for a companion), **Texas Chainsaw Massacre 2**, and **Black Widow**, and he also starred as a basketball coach driven to success in the more commercial **Hoosiers**. His work rate has barely let up since, although it seems that sobriety has somewhat killed his muse, forcing him to satisfy financial rather than artistic cravings. In the '90s, Hopper has done a roaring trade playing stock villains in such studio shlock as **Speed**, **Super Mario Bros**, **Boiling Point** and **Waterworld**, although his performances in **Paris Trout** (1991) and (a brilliant cameo) in the Tarantino-scripted **True Romance** (Tony Scott, 1993) remind us of his true talent.

Hopper's latter-day directorial efforts have also been, generally, less than inspired. **The Hot Spot** (1990) was a noir thriller starring Don Johnson that barely simmered, while the less said the better about **Chasers** (1994), a sex comedy starring Tom Berenger. **Colors** (1988), a slick drive-by of contemporary L.A. gang culture starring Sean Penn and Robert Duvall, was heavy on words, slow on drama, but imbued with a raw integrity. **Catchfire** (1989), starring Jodie Foster and Hopper himself, was the most interesting of the lot and littered with modern art references. But in a spat with the studio, it was taken out of his control, re-edited and released as "an Alan Smithee film". So perhaps it's fitting that Hopper's new clean-cut image makes a cameo in a car ad; a post-modern inheritor of all the avant-garde techniques and marketing savvy that he introduced to Hollywood.

NOTES

1. "Citizen Hopper" by Chris Hodenfield (*Film Comment*, Dec. 1986, p.62).

2. "Citizen Hopper" by Chris Hodenfield (*Film Comment*, Dec. 1986, p.64).

3. "Our Local Correspondents: Afternoons With Hopper" by James Stevenson (*New Yorker* 13-11-71, p.122).

4. "Our Local Correspondents: Afternoons With Hopper" by James Stevenson (*New Yorker* 13-11-71, p.124).

5. John Gilmore, *Laid Bare* (Amok Books, 1997, p.231).

6. Peter Fonda, *Don't Tell Dad* (Hyperion, 1998, p.256–257).

7. "Our Local Correspondents: Afternoons With Hopper" by James Stevenson (*New Yorker* 13-11-71, p.117).

8. Elena Rodriguez, *Dennis Hopper: A Madness To His Method* (St. Martin's Press, 1988).

"A KINGDOM BY THE SEA": 'NIGHT TIDE' AND THE STORY OF THE SIREN

"And so all the night tide, I lay down by the side,
Of my darling, my darling, my life and my bride
In her sepulchre there by the sea,
In her tomb by the sounding sea."
—Edgar Allan Poe, *Annabel Lee*

In **Night Tide**, Johnny Drake (Dennis Hopper) is a lonely sailor stationed in an unnamed seaside port (the film is actually shot in Malibu, Santa Monica, and Venice Beach, California). One night, visiting a dark jazz club, he meets a beautiful young girl (Linda Lawson) who's being harassed by a mysterious older woman (Cameron[1]) who speaks to her only in Greek. Disturbed by the old lady, the girl leaves the club and allows Johnny to walk her home. He discovers that her name is Mora, and she lives above the carousel in a fairground at the end of the pier. The following morning, he meets her for a fish breakfast and accompanies her to the fairground sideshow where she works as "Mora the Mermaid", sitting in a glass water-tank wearing a fish's tail. The two begin to date, and Johnny becomes strangely intrigued by this mysterious girl, especially when the fairground workers warn him that her previous two boyfriends drowned after last being seen swimming at sea with Mora.

In an effort to find out more about her, Johnny pays a visit to Mora's "keeper" and stepfather, a retired English sea captain called Sam Murdock (Gavin Muir). Captain Murdock tells Johnny that he rescued Mora as a child from a strange race of sea-people living on a Greek island; he claims that she's a siren, a "monster", fatal to men and destined finally to return to her people in the sea. When Johnny confronts Mora with this claim, she admits it to be true, despite his attempts to convince her that such things are impossible. He visits a fortune teller who informs him that he's in grave danger. The next time he goes to see Mora he falls asleep while she's in the bath, and wakes up to find that she's vanished into the sea under the pier; Johnny manages to rescue her just in time.

A few days later, Johnny and Mora go skin-diving. There's a serious struggle underwater as Mora seems to be trying to pull Johnny down; he manages to escape at the last minute, and Mora swims off alone. She never returns. Johnny goes back to his hotel to try and understand what's happening to him. Eventually, he decides to visit Mora at work for an explanation, but when he enters her sideshow booth on the pier, he finds her fish-tailed body lying in its tank, dead. Suddenly, Captain Murdock bursts into the booth and claims Johnny has murdered Mora and must pay. The captain fires a gun at him but misses, and Johnny manages to escape and alert the police.

When interviewed by the police, Captain Murdock confesses that he's always been in love with Mora and couldn't face the thought of her leaving, so told her the legend of the sea people to keep her with him forever. He admits to the murders of her two previous boyfriends, and to convincing Mora she'd killed them herself under the influence of the mysterious sea people. When Mora met Johnny, however, Captain Murdock admits his "experiment in psychology failed", since Mora decided to "embrace the rapture of the depths" rather than allowing Johnny to be killed like the others. Johnny is released by the police, and leaves in the company of Ellen (Luana Anders), a friend from the fairground.

FISH TALES

Night Tide (written and directed by Curtis Harrington[2], 1963) is a fascinating re-telling of a very traditional myth, full of interesting new takes on ancient symbols, archetypal conceits and old motifs. It isn't the first film to re-tell the story of the siren – earlier versions include **Mr. Peabody And The Mermaid** (1948), with Ann Blyth, **Mad About Men** (1954), with Glynis Johns, and **Mare Motto** (1963), with Dominique Bosquero. And nor is it the last, more recent versions including **The Glass Bottom Boat** (1966), with Doris Day, and **Splash** (1984), starring Daryl Hannah. It is, however, perhaps the most serious, understated, imagistic and elegiac re-telling of this most ancient of tales.

"Mora the Mermaid! Alive!", promise the brightly coloured sideshow posters on the pier. "Mora, ladies and gentlemen, Mora the Mermaid!" declares Captain Murdock in his showman's pitch. "The strangest creature in captivity! See her alive! See her living under water! Half-woman, half-fish – the strangest creature in captivity! For twenty-five cents, ladies and gentlemen! A quarter of a dollar! The thrill of your life, Mora the Mermaid...."

Mora is advertised alongside the Hall of Mirrors, Dr. Pink's House of Freaks, the Fun Palace, the Tunnel of Amour, the Shoot-the-Chute and the Whirlwind Racer. Mermaid exhibits were not unusual in seaside carnivals and travelling shows in the mid to late nineteenth century, though may have seemed somewhat dated as late as 1963. Unlike Mora, however, these exhibits were very rarely claimed to be "Alive!". A siren purportedly found by a group of Malaysians and then sold and exhibited in London in 1832 as a

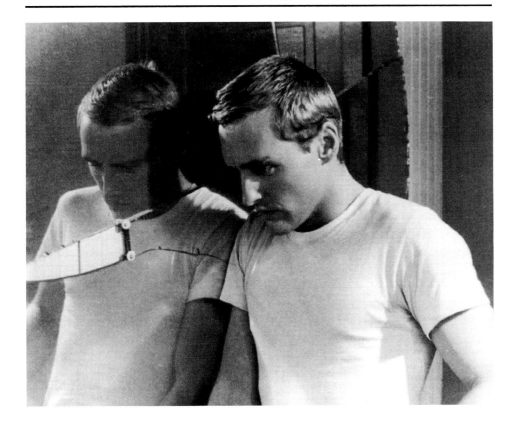

sideshow attraction was revealed to be composed of the upper part of a female monkey and the lower part of a tuna. Barnum advertised a "Living Mermaid" or "Fascinating Fish Woman" in the mid nineteenth century, said to have been "authenticated by reputable scientists as native of the Fiji Islands, which were at that time the last stronghold of cannibalism". But Barnum's mermaid turned out to be an ape's body attached to a fish's tail, and was eventually put on display in the Boston museum.

THE KNIGHT OF CUPS

Hopper plays the role of Johnny Drake with a quiet and precise restraint. Johnny is a shy and lonely sailor, awkward, laconic, inexperienced, slightly simple. He doesn't really believe there are such things as mermaids, yet is mesmerized by Mora, and the stories he hears about her. He doesn't believe in fortune-telling either, but ends up sitting in the tent of the clairvoyant (Marjorie Eaton). His father left his mother when Johnny was very young, he tells Mora quietly, and when his mother died he decided to join the navy to "see the world", though he confesses sadly that he hasn't seen much of it yet. He was brought up by his mother, to whom he was very close.

Johnny seems strangely fascinated by Mora's fake fish-tail, which appears in his dreams. He seems mesmerized by her dangerous seductiveness, her phallic power. Yet at the same time, something about her terrifies him – he also has dreams about being strangled by a monstrous octopus composed of fish-tails. And yet despite his modest, shuffling, unpolished nature, he's the first man in Mora's life powerful enough to challenge her preternatural strength.

What is interesting and in some ways unique about Hopper's performance in **Night Tide** is the fact that his character remains so quiet, so laconic, so underplayed. This is particularly notable since the film was made at a time when Hopper was quickly gaining the reputation of being a selfish and temperamental actor[3] who seemed to have absorbed all the causeless rebellion of his friend James Dean, who died in 1955. **Night Tide** gives us the opportunity to see Hopper in an uncharacteristically low-key role, playing a character who is neither gritty, wild, menacing nor psychotic, but pensive, thoughtful, sometimes rather slow on the uptake.

In the role of Johnny, Hopper is calm and silent, a mother's boy. **Night Tide** is an aberration in Hopper's usual repertoire of sweaty, eye-rolling performances; certainly, Johnny bears no resemblance whatsoever to the gallery of middle-aged oddballs, freaks and psychos that Hopper plays so adeptly in later movies like **River's Edge**, **Blue Velvet** and **Paris Trout**. In these later films, Hopper is typically ruthless, cruel, raving, but Johnny gives us no indication of this psychotic, self-absorbed character that Hopper was eventually to typecast himself as. Nor does **Night Tide** provide a filmic showcase – as many of these later films do – of the off-screen Dennis Hopper – a man from whom, as Peter Biskind claims in a recent book, people walked in genuine fear of their lives.

THE MERMAID

Mora is a coy and beautiful young woman who is obsessed with the sea. Her apartment is decorated with treasures from the ocean and seashore – seaweed, shells, starfish. Her favourite food, she tells Johnny, is seafood – mackerel, lobster, crab and sea urchin. "To you, me and the beautiful Pacific," she toasts him. Seagulls fly into her lap and sit there quietly, allowing her to play with them like pets. Her voice is seductive and enchanting, her appearance suggests purity, sophistication, enlightenment. Like the siren of myth and legend, she tempts Johnny by diverting him away from his old life, his past experiences and institutions. Mora holds the promise of something outside Johnny's world of everyday disillusions and disappointments. Her effect is to seduce, meaning literally to lead elsewhere, to divert, to lead

astray, to deviate, shift, change course – actions that all belong to the secret and ritual, given that what seduces is not obvious but covert and hidden.

One of the things that most fascinates Johnny about Mora is her asexual quality, her seeming purity. His self-confessed closeness to his mother has perhaps created in him a certain amount of anxiety about female sexuality, since what appeals to him about Mora is her ambiguous and contradictory nature. And the siren, of course, lacks female genital organs. In her role as the mermaid, Mora's upper body awakens a desire that her lower parts are incapable of satisfying. She's a metaphor of the impenetrable female made literal. To Johnny, she's a disturbing object of attraction and anguish.

Another of Mora's seductive features is her long, dark mermaid's hair. As Johnny should know, sailors have a number of superstitions regarding hair, and it wasn't unheard of for a sailor to forbid his wife or lover to cut her hair while he was away at sea. According to a similar nautical superstition, Mora's name is an unlucky one because it ends in the letter "A". Sailors believe that names ending in the letter "A" bring bad luck, and this is why so few vessels have these kinds of names (many claim that the Lusitania, lost on May 7th 1915, was a perfect example of this superstition at work).

Like all mermaids, Mora is considered to be dangerous – to use her charms to lure unwary sailors like Johnny into dangerous waters. "Mora is quite dangerous," Captain Murdock tells Johnny, who frowns and shifts around uncomfortably in his seat. "Let's say she suffers from a certain compulsion that might cause her to try and take your life," he continues. "Break off this acquaintance before it's too late. You're a nice fellow. I wouldn't like to see you get hurt." Johnny grows increasingly awkward and ill at ease.

The clairvoyant tells him a similar story. "Take a good look at these cards, young man," she says, indicating the tarot deck spread out on the table before her. "They represent all the secrets of the universe." Johnny himself is represented as the Knight of Cups, the innocent and searching young man. His present state is symbolized by the Moon card, featuring a crab attempting to climb out of the water and on to the shore, but being constantly drawn back again. His future is the Hanged Man, representing a life in suspension, a deep entrancement.

"But what about Mora?" he asks the Clairvoyant, confused.

"I'm afraid she's in a vortex of evil," the woman replies. "And you? It pains me to tell you, but you're in danger, grave danger."

"What kind of danger?" frowns Johnny.

"Now, that is a question you do not need to ask me," replies the fortune teller. "The answer lies already in your heart."

"You certainly know the legend of the sirens? The sirens were a strange race of people, half-human, half-creatures of the sea," Captain Murdock tells him, later on. Johnny gives him a cynical look. "You wouldn't believe they actually exist, would you?" counters Murdock. "Where do you think myths come from? Do you think they're just made up? No! They spring from truth, ancient truth, living truth!"

THE MOON, THE SEA, THE TIDES

As they walk together along the beach, Mora tells Johnny that Captain Murdock discovered her as a child living in the sun amongst the sea-people on the island of Mikolos. "You love the sun, don't you?" he asks her.

"Yes," replies Mora. "The sun, the moon and the stars..."

"And the sea."

"Yes. Yes, the sea. I love the sea most of all. But I guess I'm a little afraid of it, too."

Like the siren she believes herself to be, Mora is obsessed by the sea. She keeps a conical shell with her, to have the sound of the ocean close by at all times; she lives in "Ocean View Apartments"; she loves to take long, deep baths, and feels the sea constantly urging her to come home. "I feel the sea water in my veins," she tells Johnny. "The tide pulls at my heart."

Many people once believed that the souls of the dead migrate to those mysterious areas beyond the sea's horizon. The sea has a duel nature – it represents purification, regeneration and perpetuity, but it can also be destructive, causing inundation, shipwreck, drowning and annihilation. In the Germanic languages, the words "sea" and "soul" have the same root. And according to Gaston Bachelard, "water dies with the dead in its substance. Water is then a substantial nothingness. No-one can go further in despair than this. For certain souls, water is the matter of despair".

Mora also confesses to Johnny that "the face of the moon" fills her with "a strange longing". Captain Murdock tells Johnny he has to be particularly careful with Mora around the time of the full moon, because "that's when the tide pulls the strongest". Sailors in most seafaring countries believed the moon to have special powers. Many thought the moon to be a goddess, associating her with the goddesses of the sea.

Like the siren of myth and legend, Mora is considered to be responsible for the destruction of previous men, who apparently abandoned their courses and threw themselves into the waters in order to get close to her. The path to her bedroom is strewn with corpses. Ellen, the daughter of the man who owns the Merry-Go-Round, gives Johnny the lowdown on Mora's cursed past. "In the past two years," she tells him, "Mora's had two boyfriends, and they're both dead now... They were both nice boys and they went around with her. Now they're both dead – their bodies found washed up, on shore... if she didn't cause those deaths, she brings bad luck, which is just as bad."

In ancient times, many sailors refused to learn to swim because they believed that the destiny of those who were taken by the sea was to drown, and attempting swimming was blasphemy. Others believed that to save a drowning man would anger the gods of the sea, who would then exact vengeance on the rescuers. Many sailors were averse to water, claiming that to go swimming would be to tempt the spirits of the sea, who would hunger thereafter for the swimmer to return. Johnny, however, is a strong swimmer. When Mora sleepwalks into the ocean he rescues her from the fierce waves underneath the pier. And when she takes him by boat to the open sea to go diving in the reefs looking for treasures, he, unlike Mora, manages to escape from the fatal currents of the deep.

The siren of myth and legend traditionally drags the unfortunate sailor down to her underwater abyss, and it seems for a moment that this is what Mora intends to do to Johnny. It soon becomes clear, however, that she is as much at the mercy of the waves as he is, and, where Johnny survives, Mora finally gives herself over to the powers of the sea. As the story tells us, the siren is never strong enough to survive the first man to resist her. Defeated, she's seized by a self-destructive urge powerful enough for her to fall to the bottom of the ocean, a dead weight.

BIRDS AND SHADOWS

There is a rather enigmatic and threatening note to **Night Tide**, enhanced by the impressionistic cinematography of Vilis Lapenieks. The hallway that leads to Mora's apartment is full of mysterious shadows; the strange feel of the final scenes on the pier is produced by irregular strikes of lightning in the skies. Things happen that can't be explained – Johnny gets a telephone call on the merry-go-round when no-one knows he's there, and there's no-one on the other end of the line; the old Greek woman leads him to Captain Murdock's house, then seemingly vanishes. A rocking-chair rocks apparently of its own accord; washing waves on a line, even though there is no breeze. Johnny's dreams of Mora segue into reality. Captain Murdock keeps stuffed wild animals and a cabinet full of curiosities, including a severed hand preserved in pickle ("a little Arabian souvenir, the hand of a thief... a little gift from the Sultan of Marrakech").

This edgy feeling is perfected by the use of symbolism in the film, notably symbolism to do with birds. Many scenes are backed by the cries of seagulls. Mora has a special affinity with these birds. Whilst eating breakfast on the balcony, she summons one of the birds which lands beside her on the table. She puts it in her lap and strokes it like a pet – something she learned to do, she claims, on the Greek island where she was born. Johnny seems to have something in common with these birds. He, too, is irresistibly drawn to Mora. Johnny's surname is the name of a bird: Drake.

Due to their mournful sounding cries, most seabirds were believed to be the lost souls of drowned sailors, and their cries were thought to be voices in torment. Some sailors believed in the myth that birds carried human souls, and they were consequently very reluctant to harm them. Others believed that when a bird hovered over their ship, it meant that someone on board was about to die. The predictions of the fortune teller seem to reinforce this omen. "The cards will tell you a great deal," she says to Johnny, cryptically. And yet the death anticipated in this case is not that of Johnny, as his tarot hand seems to imply, but rather that of his enchantress, Mora.

THE SONG OF THE SIREN

One important aspect of the traditional tale of the siren that might at first seems to be missing in **Night Tide** is music. Legend has it that the siren draws sailors to their deaths through the power of her irresistible song, an

unearthly, enchanting music that sways the senses. In **Night Tide**, this intoxicating music is the sound of the carousel above which Mora lives, and whose haunting sound draws Johnny back to her over and over again. She chooses to live above the merry-go-round, she tells Johnny, because "its music reminds me of when I was a child". The music of the carousel provides an evocative background to many of the scenes in Mora's apartment, but also occurs non-diegetically elsewhere – in the scene where Johnny follows the mysterious Greek woman, for example, and the scene in which he has his fortune told by the "clairomancer". It also seems significant that the last we see of Johnny, he's returning to the merry-go-round with Ellen, the daughter with its owner.

There is other haunting music in the film, too, as well as the song of the carousel. Johnny is first drawn to Mora when he spots her in The Blue Grotto, a jazz club. When he tries to talk to her she asks him to be quiet, mesmerized by the music ("Seaweed" by Jimmy Bond, and – echoing the Poe line from which the film's title is taken – "The Tell-Tale Harp" by David Raksin). A few days later, while walking on the beach, Mora and Johnny meet a group of bongo drummers who persuade Mora to dance for them. The drumming begins slowly; Mora dances slowly and seductively, but as the pace of the music increases she seems to be growing hypnotized, dancing as though she's in some kind of trance, performing a frantic tarantella, until she finally collapses on the ground in an exhausted faint.

Other notable background sounds in the movie include the cries of seagulls, the faint shouts of children playing, church bells and high-pitched flute music. We also hear the faint barking of dogs and the clucking of chickens, the noise of traffic, ships' sirens, the note of distant thunder, and, always gently and persistently, the sound of the sea.

MYTH, DREAMS AND LEGENDS

The mystery of **Night Tide** is purportedly solved when Captain Murdock confesses to having murdered Mora's previous two boyfriends to keep her for himself. "I've loved her ever since I found her," he weeps. "I couldn't face the thought of her leaving, so I decided to plan some way to keep her with me always." He convinced Mora that she was one of an ancient race of sea-people, and was waiting for the time when she would be called back to the sea.

But Johnny still has a question he needs answering: who was the mysterious Greek woman who first brought he and Mora together, and who led him to the home of Captain Murdock? Mora once told him she was one of the sea people. "She's one of them, Johnny," she told him, "...and she's here to remind me of the time I must go to them, to the sea." Before leaving the police station, Johnny asks Captain Murdock who the Greek woman really was, but he seems to have no knowledge of her. "There wasn't any woman," he tells Johnny. "I don't know what you're talking about."

In the fairytale world of **Night Tide**, the old Greek woman functions as a style of transitional object – the souvenir brought back into the "real" world from the land of dreams. The transitional object proves, in a very special way, that the dream was not completely a fantasy, that it had an element of truth to it that remains inexplicable and mysterious. But the identity of the old woman is not the only aspect of Johnny's dream that remains unresolved. There are other questions that are left without answers.

If Mora spent her childhood on a remote and deserted Greek island, why does she claim that the music of the merry-go-round reminds her of when she was a child? When Johnny spots a newspaper advertising the twentieth anniversary of the Amusement Pier, why is "Mora the Mermaid" listed as one of the "unique attractions" that have "continued to draw crowds" for the last twenty years? Captain Murdock, paraphrasing Hamlet, tells Johnny at one point that "things happen in this world never dreamt of in your philosophy".

But perhaps Mora puts it best of all. "Americans have such a simple view of the world," she tells Johnny, when they're walking one day on the beach. "You think you've discovered reality, but you don't even know what it is."

NOTES

1. Marjorie Cameron, a poet and artist also known for her roles as The Scarlet Woman and Kali in Kenneth Anger's **Inauguration Of The Pleasure Dome** (1954), in which **Night Tide**'s director Curtis Harrington also appears, as Cesare, the somnambulist from **The Cabinet Of Dr Caligari** (1919).

2. Curtis Harrington began as an underground film-maker, producing such movies as **Fragment Of Seeking** (1946), **On The Edge** (1949) and an 8mm version of Edgar Allan Poe's **Fall Of The House Of Usher**, made when he was a boy. His later, mainstream films include **What's The Matter With Helen?** (1971), **The Killing Kind** (1973), and **Ruby** (1977). **Night Tide** may be seen as a transitional film between these two bodies of work, transposing the mythological and psychosexual concerns of an "underground" text onto a B-movie framework; as such it is probably his most interesting work.

3. Hopper had been dismissed from Henry Hathaway's **From Hell To Texas**, reputedly with the director's assurance that Hopper would never work in Hollywood again. Lean years indeed followed, during which Hopper's acting roles were largely limited to exploitation pictures such as **Queen Of Blood** (again directed by Curtis Harrington), Anthony M Lanza's **The Glory Stompers**, and Roger Corman's **The Trip**.

"TOMBSTONES IN THEIR EYES": 'EASY RIDER' AND THE DEATH OF THE AMERICAN DREAM

"You know I've seen a lot of people walkin' round
With tombstones in their eyes,
But the pusher don't care
If you live or if you die"
　　　　　—Steppenwolf, "The Pusher"

Produced for less than $400,000, **Easy Rider** premiered at Cannes in 1969, where it was shown in competition, and would also have been included in the New York Film Festival had Columbia not opted for a summer release. Hailed by *Time* as "one of the ten most important pictures of the decade", the film grossed at least $40 million, winning approval from critics, and limitless enthusiasm from audiences. It earned Hopper a special award from the National Society of Film Critics, an Oscar nomination for Best Original Screenplay, and, for Jack Nicholson, a nomination for Best Supporting Actor. Both critically, commercially and financially, **Easy Rider** is by far one of the most successful films of the last thirty years, and every generation since its initial release, Hopper's wild tale of drugs, dreams and rock'n'roll has still managed to find a cult following. But the power of this unconventional classic lies not in its facile crucifixion tale of the loving beatniks destroyed by a corrupt and backward society, but in Hopper's radical fusion of a hip, acid-drenched psychedelic road movie with some very traditional western themes and motifs.

　　Anybody who knows anything about the life and career of Dennis Hopper will be familiar with his compulsive fascination for western myths. This fascination can be traced back to the time and place of his birth – Hopper was born in Dodge City, Kansas, in 1936, exactly sixty years after Wyatt Earp was brought in to clean up the town and pacify its rowdy outlaws, and three years before Warner Brothers celebrated that event with a vehicle for Errol Flynn (**Dodge City**, 1939). Most of the movies Hopper has directed may be viewed as crypto-westerns (**Easy Rider** 1969; **The Last Movie** 1971; **Out Of The Blue** 1980; **Colors** 1988; **Catchfire** 1989; **The Hot Spot** 1990) filled with guns, outlaws, shoot-ups and plenty of wild west mayhem. In those he appears in himself, Hopper often wears a trademark cowboy hat, as though compensating for the oversized Stetson his on-screen father humiliated him with in George Stevens's **Giant** (1956)[1].

　　The heroes of **Easy Rider** are two part-time drug-dealing motorcyclists

named, appropriately enough, Wyatt, or Captain America (Peter Fonda), and Billy (Hopper). The calm Fonda, with his gleaming silver-chromed, low-riding motorcycle, wears tight leather pants with a huge western-style belt-buckle, a black leather jacket with an American flag on the back, and a stars-and-stripes helmet. His bike has a stars-and-stripes teardrop gas tank[2], in which the pair keep their drug money, rolled up and concealed inside a long plastic tube. Hopper, in contrast, restless as a child, sports long hair, thick sideburns and a droopy moustache, and is dressed more like Wild Bill Hickcock than Billy the Kid, in a Stetson and fringed buckskin jacket, with a necklace made from animals' teeth.

"EACH MAN IS A LEADER..."

Like their counterparts in the traditional western, both Fonda and Hopper are loners, excluded not only from any manifestations of domesticity, but also from any potential erotic or romantic encounters.

Their first stop is at a traditional horse ranch, where Fonda needs to repair a flat tire on his bike (in juxtaposition to a real cowboy, who's shoeing his horse in the same barn). The rancher invites them to stay for dinner, and they sit at a long, outdoor dining table with the rancher, his Mexican wife, and their many Mexican-American children. Fonda seems deeply envious of the situation ("nice spread", he says, approvingly, "you've got a nice place... you should be proud"), and yet at the same time seems restless, and eager to move on. The domestic scene is somehow both attractive and yet somehow alienating to him.

A similar situation occurs in the hippie commune at which a hitchhiker, known only as Stranger (Luke Askew), wishes to be dropped. Pleased to be home at last, he grabs a woman, kisses her, and plays with some of the hippie children; Fonda and Hopper stay for dinner, but are clearly not welcome to stay ("we just can't take any more," one of the women complains, "...just too many people dropping in"). In exchange for the food they've just eaten, the drug-dealing beatniks give a lift "over across the canyon" on their bikes to two of the hippie girls, Sarah (Sabrina Scharf) and Lisa (Luana Anders[3]), who's taken a liking to Fonda. The foursome walk along the bank of a stream, then shed their clothes and go swimming together in a rock grotto. Again, Fonda is envious of the "spread" and seems tempted to stay and develop a relationship with Lisa, but as usual, Hopper is frantically, manically restless, and manages to compel his pal to return to their journey. "Man, look," he says, "I gotta get out of here, man. Now, we – we got things we want to do, man, like – I just – uh – I gotta get out of here, man").

It also seems significant that by the time they reach Madame Tinkertoy's brothel in New Orleans, both men are too strung out to have any use for the two prostitutes they hook up with (Toni Basil and Karen Black) except to split a tab of acid with them. This exclusion from the erotic and the domestic is a typical hallmark of the conventional cowboy hero (think of John Wayne in **The Searchers**, for example).

Another hallmark of the traditional western hero is his ambiguous relationship with the law, leading to much uncertainty over issues of identity, which seems rather ironic for such a stalwart, archetypal figure as the cowboy. Nothing could be truer of Hopper and Fonda in **Easy Rider**. Their costumes mark them out at one and the same time as freaks, heads, and genuine patriotic Americans. They are both "good guys" and drug-dealing criminals. After filling both bike tanks with gas at an Enco station, they ride off without paying, even though they are rich with drug money. As they leave, the last shot cuts to the gas station building, where a poor Mexican girl looks out through the window.

This ambiguity seems particularly relevant in Hopper's case. He dresses like an Indian, in animal skins and a necklace made of teeth (though sporting a cowboy hat at the same time), and at the commune he plays cowboys and indians with the hippie children, yelling "bang bang!" as he exchanges imaginary gunfire with them. Foreshadowing future events perhaps, he dives down to the ground, crying out "pow pow pow ppttwang, you can't hit me,

I'm invisible, I'm invisible!", and yet a big glob of mud hits him right in the center of his chest.

Later on, of course, the two outlaws get thrown in jail for "parading without a permit", and Hopper angrily and vehemently pleads his innocence and patriotism as the jail cell door is closed on him. "You gotta be kidding!" he shouts, aggressively. "I mean, do you know who this is, man? This is Captain America. I'm Billy. Hey, we're headliners, baby. We played every fair in this part of the country. I mean, for top dollar, too!" It seems ironic that the friend Hopper and Fonda make in prison turns out to be a lawyer, George Hanson (Jack Nicholson), a synthesizing combination of liberal and conservative ideals. Nicholson plays the languid, drunken scion of a wealthy, southern family, whose bizarre drinking ritual parodies a cowboy catchphrase (he swigs down Jim Beam with his elbow flapping at his side like a chicken, chanting "nik-nik-nik-f-f-f-Indians!").

As soon as Nicholson joins the restless duo, he is identified as one of them, at least in the eyes of the local rednecks, who have them down simply as "troublemakers" and "weirdo degenerates" ("you name it, I throw rocks at it, Sheriff", says one of them to another, lasciviously). It's Nicholson who articulates the prophetic theme of the film – the bikers' threat to the Establishment and to Americans who are hypocritical about the repressive materialism of their society and culture. Hopper claims resentfully that their beat costumes and long hair spark intolerance, but Nicholson explains that they actually represent something deeper and more fearful – freedom, experimentation, and a rejection of the entrapments of capitalist society. It seems ironic, then, that it's Nicholson who's ultimately beaten to death by the local assassins, since he – as a lawyer from a wealthy family – has much more in common with the ambushers than either Hopper or Fonda.

This confusion and ambiguity over identity is, in fact, cleverly foreshadowed in Nicholson's earlier marijuana-fuelled campfire speech about aliens from the planet Venus. His "crackpot idea" is that Venutians have already landed on earth and are living amongst us, working as ordinary people. These aliens are indistinguishable from normal human beings except, Hanson tells us, that they "don't have no wars, they got no monetary system, they don't have any leaders, because, I mean, each man is a leader". Many critics and audience members claim that **Easy Rider** used the social context of the period to express discontent towards the status quo. But in fact the identities of Fonda and Hopper in this film, and their relationship to the rest of society, becomes so fluid and ambiguous that they somehow lose some of their individuality. This allows us to see them, perhaps, more as iconic images of the late 1960s than as personalities in their own right.

"ALL CITIES ARE ALIKE..."

Perhaps the most immediately recognizable theme of the traditional western is its use of landscape. **Easy Rider**'s fusion of the landscape of the American west with the hallucinatory visual experience of the road movie is a touch of sheer genius on Hopper's part. One of the earliest road movies (a logical extension of the motor-psychedelic youth flick), **Easy Rider** is perhaps the quintessential archetype of the genre. It charts a continually changing cinematic landscape across the windswept vistas of Arizona's Monument Valley, the setting for countless western classics of the 1950s and '60s, especially those starring John Wayne.

Instead of the traditional epic quest, however, Hopper blows our minds with this reckless joyride of uneven pacing, mesmeric jump-cuts by Laszlo Kovacs, flash-forward transitions between scenes, and background rock'n'roll to complement the narrative. Critic Andrew Sarris complained in the *Village Voice* that "with all the rousingly rhythmic revelry and splendiferously scenic motorcycling, **Easy Rider** comes to resemble a perpetual pre-credit sequence"[4], but other critics were far more appreciative.

Unlike the traditional western, whose theme is the founding of civilizations, **Easy Rider** leads us in search of the entropic disorder of the wilderness, far from the smug repression of urban culture. Or, in the words

of the Stranger:

"It doesn't make any difference what city. All cities are alike. That's why I'm out here now... cause I'm from the city, a long way from the city – and that's where I want to be right now."

And again, in a clever inversion of western motifs, rather than travelling westward on horses to push through the frontier, Fonda and Hopper travel eastward from Los Angeles – the end of the traditional frontier – on Harley Davidson choppers, on an epic journey into the unknown, to escape from civilization. In fact, in interviews, Hopper has repeatedly stressed that this reverse trajectory, from west to east, is symbolic of the fact that Wyatt and Billy are representatives of a fundamentally criminal society, and embody a seductive, spurious freedom. Rather than offering a revisionist view of American history, **Easy Rider** is an inverse, regressive western, a story of betrayed ideals, a futile, anti-epic quest for a non-existent past.

"MISFORTUNE AND DESPAIR"

Despite all the energy and inspiration of Hopper's powerful directing and antsy performance, **Easy Rider** remains a remarkable bleak and downbeat film, reflecting only too vividly the collapse of the ideals of the 1960s. It seems rather significant, in retrospect, that the film was released in the same year as the Manson murders, that other oft-cited marker of "the death of the sixties". Hopper tells Fonda again and again that what he's searching for is "the American Dream", and as the duo enter the open hinterlands and degenerate backwaters between cities, it becomes increasingly clear that this ideal is no more than a conceit, an illusion. What Hopper seems to embody, in fact, is nothing more than restlessness, existential angst, dissatisfaction, the quest for the next fix, for further and further kicks.

The dream Hopper seems to be searching for is, in fact, the road itself, which seems to run in a circle and end in carnage, mayhem, abject lawlessness and dead-end fatalism. In other words, there's no new frontier to be crossed, no new landscape to be discovered, nowhere to explore except the psychosocial wasteland of those for whom personal and national identity have become meaningless.

According to critic Michael Atkinson, Billy's restless angst and his itchy compulsion to chase his own tail have become significant hallmarks of the road movie post-**Easy Rider**:

"In the road movie we have an ideogram of human desire and last-ditch search for self... Predicated for the most part on despair, heartbreak and

post-noir melancholia, road trips never end as we hope and instead thrust us into an environment ruled by misfortune and raw jungle hate... Whatever might be found on the road, it won't resemble any universal truth, it will elude those explicitly searching for it, and it won't be easy to tie to the hood and bring home[5]."

This feeling of loss and rootlessness is nowhere more clear in **Easy Rider** than in the extended graveyard acid trip sequence at the end of the movie, where the film really seems to lose its way (perhaps reflecting the fact that these were actually the first, scriptless scenes shot). For Fonda, this experience seals his suspicion that the whole trip has been deeply dissatisfying, transitory, and elusive, whereas the naïve, less meditative Hopper remains unaware of the cost of their trip to his own soul. Hopper feels that the two have succeeded in their quest for the "big money", but Fonda suspects there might have been another, less destructive, more spiritually fulfilling way to find freedom than selling hard drugs, taking to the road, getting sidetracked and wasting their lives.

"We blew it," he tells Hopper in the final campfire scene, and you get the sense that he's talking about more than just their acid trip, or even their

drug deal or their journey to New Orleans. Hopper, edgy as ever, repeatedly asks him what he means, but Fonda remains enigmatic. In fact, as director, Hopper allegedly wanted Wyatt to clarify and explain this line, but Fonda refused to do so. "I didn't want to," he says, now. "I simply wanted to say, in an enigmatic way, 'we blew it', and leave it there... – what did he mean, 'we blew it'? Where? It remains enigmatic as hell. And that means you have to go back and back and back and try to figure it out..."[6].

AFTERMATH

In some ways, perhaps, they did blow it. The enormous financial success of **Easy Rider** caused a significant and lasting rift in the friendship between Fonda and Hopper, who have never agreed on the appropriate division of the film's proceeds. Hopper apparently received only 7% of the $40 million the film grossed, and alleges that according to a verbal agreement with Fonda, he should have got half, but never did. Hopper is currently claiming, through his lawyer, to have written the entire script alone.

According to the *Wall Street Journal* where the story was first reported, the real trouble is ego-driven. Fonda has never had a big hit since **Easy Rider**, and for a number of years has, reportedly, been attempting to get Hopper to agree to a sequel starring his daughter, Bridget. Hopper has apparently consistently refused to contemplate the idea. His own memories of directing **Easy Rider** are apparently not good ones. He blames the film for the break-up of his first marriage to model Brooke Hayward, daughter of Margaret Sullivan and, incidentally, a childhood friend of Peter Fonda.

Significantly, the rejection of a capitalist ideology espoused by Hopper's character in **Easy Rider** never seems to have influenced his attitude toward the film's proceeds and dividends. Or perhaps he too espoused more egalitarian ideals at an earlier time, but they turned out to be as illusory as the mythical American Dream. At any rate, whatever Hopper intended to discover or achieve through the production of **Easy Rider** seems constantly have eluded him. Or, as the famous ad-line put it, "A man went searching for America – and couldn't find it anywhere..."

NOTES

1. See J. Hoberman, *Dennis Hopper: From Method To Madness*, Walker Art Center Film/Video exhibition program, Walker Art Center, Minneapolis, 1988.

2. A much-copied design, which apparently may soon become illegal, due to the U.S. government's recent plans to strengthen the laws about flag desecration.

3. Who plays Ellen in Hopper's earlier movie, **Night Tide** (1961).

4. Andrew Sarris, *Village Voice*, cit in Hoberman, 15.

5. Michael Atkinson, "Crossing The Frontiers", *Sight & Sound* November 1992, p14-17.

6. Peter Fonda interview, *Microsoft Cinemania*, **Easy Rider**.

"UNSPEAKABLE RITES": DENNIS HOPPER AND 'THE LAST MOVIE'

"Show me the stones the builders have rejected, for they are the cornerstones."

(—Epigram in the movie-set church, **The Last Movie**)

Dennis Hopper's **The Last Movie** is an experimental film consisting of three complicated, interlocking narratives. The first story concerns a Hollywood western about Billy the Kid, directed by Sam Fuller on location in Peru, during which the actor playing Billy (Dean Stockwell) is accidentally shot. The second story involves the stunt man, Kansas (Dennis Hopper), who decides to stay behind in Peru after the rest of the film crew has left, moving in with an ex-prostitute named Maria. Kansas builds himself a Malibu-style home on a mountain top, in the hope of developing Chincheros as a production site for future western movies. He also gets involved with a fellow American who's seeking funds to finance his dream quest for a gold mine. The final story involves the local Indians who, having watched the shooting of Fuller's western with fascination, now re-stage it as a totemic ritual on the abandoned set. Reversing the original cinematic procedure, the Indians use make-believe equipment to "document" actual violence, including the death of Kansas, who's selected to die in the "movie", and imprisoned to await his sentence.

"ENDLESS, CHAOTIC, SUFFOCATING, ACID-SOAKED..."

Although it won a special award at the Venice Film Festival, **The Last Movie** received totally damning reviews in the U.S. when it opened in New York on September 30th 1971, and was hastily withdrawn by the distributor just two weeks later. The film was described as "hateful" (Andrew Sarris), "pure fiasco" (Judith Crist), "disaster" (William Wolf), "pitiful" (Roger Ebert), "lowest rating" (Kathleen Carroll), "an embarrassment... endless, chaotic, suffering, acid-soaked" (David Denby)[1]. The film inspired an extraordinary amount of disdain and contempt, directed both at the nature of the movie itself, and Hopper's own apparently arrogant non-conformism. As Robert Stam has pointed out in defense of Woody Allen's similarly vilified **Stardust Memories**, "reflexive films have often been 'bad objects' for critics, who resent the sabotage of the conventional pleasures of illusion and identification"[2].

Whatever the reasons behind the critics' violent disdain for **The Last Movie**, its reception put Hopper beyond the pale. In Hollywood, he became "an anathema, an aesthetic Charlie Manson"[3], and studio heads were quick to revoke the license they'd granted him for **Easy Rider** (1969). As a Universal Studios executive said to Hopper after the release of **The Last Movie**, "art is worth something only if you're dead. We'll only make money on this picture if you die"[4].

One factor which may have influenced the film's unfortunate critical reception was the rumours doing the rounds in Hollywood about sordid goings-on during its production. The *New York Times*, *Look*, *Playboy*, *Esquire*, *Rolling Stone* and *Life* all carried lurid accounts of drugs, parties and promiscuity on set, that established the tone for subsequent characterizations of the film as an orgy of self-indulgence, and attacks on Hopper as an out-of-control madman. "At 34," wrote Brad Darrach in *Life*, "he is known in Hollywood as a sullen renegade who talks revolution, settles arguments with karate, goes to bed with groupies and takes trips on everything you can swallow or shoot"[5].

Things got even worse when a plane full of the movie's cast scandalized a local flight crew with their blatant marijuana-smoking. As a result, the CIA was said to be monitoring the shoot, and paranoia was endemic[6]. Darrach painted a vivid picture of wild parties, abundant drugs, easy and frenzied sex. He claimed in the article that no-one had any idea of what the movie was about or where it was leading, and characterized Hopper as a compulsive loser who often turned to drugs, and who responded to the daily pressures of directing by crying in the arms of a girlfriend at night. Thus, according to writer William Siska, "it became acceptable to respond to the finished film as if it were at best a disorganized mess, rather than attempt a synthesis of its obvious complexities"[7].

INFLUENCES: 'EASY RIDER' (1969) AND 'REBEL WITHOUT A CAUSE' (1955)

In a rather misguided attempt to enhance the film's commercial viability, **The Last Movie** was touted as "the follow-up to **Easy Rider**". In fact, it was the overwhelming financial success of **Easy Rider**, a modestly-budgeted commercial feature ($375,000), that earned for Hopper the opportunity to make a personal film free of studio interference. Rather than being a "follow-up" to the earlier film, however, **The Last Movie** takes the flamboyant imagery of **Easy Rider**'s acid trip/cemetery sequence, and extends it into an entire feature-length film. **The Last Movie** is basically composed of a series of montages whose juxtaposed sounds and abstract imagery parallel stylistically the acid trip sequence in the earlier movie; it also includes rock-scored lyrical interludes and the naturalistic use of marijuana on screen, both of which were pioneered in **Easy Rider**. And whilst editing **The Last Movie**, Hopper was reportedly studying the work of underground film-maker Bruce Conner, whose film-making techniques were also a significant influence on **Easy Rider**[8]. Claims Hopper:

"A lot of the editing in **Easy Rider** was directly influenced by seeing Bruce Conner's experimental films – the rides, the back cutting, scenes in which you're going forward but you're really going backward that I start doing at the end of the film. The things I did in the graveyard sequences came either directly from commercials that I was working on at the time, or were some sort of tribute to Bruce[9]."

Another film whose influence is less obvious but which also inflects many of the images and ideas in **The Last Movie** is Nicholas Ray's seminal 1955 movie **Rebel Without A Cause**, in which Hopper plays a minor role as a juvenile delinquent. Scenarist Stewart Stern, who co-wrote the screenplay of **The Last Movie** with Hopper, was also the writer of **Rebel Without A Cause**[10], and some critics have suggested that what impels the character of Kansas is the same motive as that which impelled Hopper to make the movie in the first place: survivor guilt. Kansas has survived the death of Billy the Kid (Dean Stockwell), just as Hopper survived the death of James Dean, and both seem to suffer from a need to embrace a martyrdom as great as that of the departed idol[11].

As a film which attempts to negotiate the boundaries between artifice and reality, **The Last Movie** is also directly influenced by Dean's method-acting philosophy. According to Hopper, Dean advised him that when he was acting, he should be real. "[H]e said, 'Do it, don't show it'", recalls Hopper. "'If you're drinking a beer, just drink it... Don't shut out what's going on around you when you're filming – accept it all as a reality, don't worry about it, learn to relax. Accept the audience as a reality – you're real, they're real, and you're the same!'"[12]

STRUCTURE, CINEMA, PSYCHODRAMA

One of the obvious complexities of **The Last Movie** involves the nexus of issues surrounding the ambiguous image of the cowboy. Several of the films directed by, and starring, Hopper are crypto-westerns, filled with guns, violence and madness. In each one, the director himself wears a trademark cowboy hat. In his early days when he was working mainly on television,

Hopper earned his living playing cowboys; in **The Last Movie**, his character, Kansas, is a lone horseman of the apocalypse, combining the image of the cowboy with that of the violent, volatile hustler. Significantly, Hopper himself was born and grew up in Dodge City, Kansas, legendary home of Billy the Kid.

In fact, much of **The Last Movie** can be regarded as Hopper's personal psychodrama – a movie about himself, his life, his fears and fetishes. It's even been suggested that Hopper unconsciously worked to turn the film into a fiasco, deliberately provoking the outrage of reviewers because "he secretly desired the chastisement of those bad notices"[13]. Those working on set commented that, as the filming progressed, Hopper seemed to become increasingly violent and full of rebellious self-pity, acting like a man who was haunted, a man who seemed sometimes even on the verge of losing his sanity. Screenwriter Stewart Stern, for example, was horrified when he saw what Hopper was doing to his script, and tried to persuade him to return to the original version. But according to Stern, Hopper was adamant. "He said 'Look. There are many movies in a movie... but this is my movie, my movie, and that's the movie that's going out on screen'"[14]. And in a documentary made while he was editing **The Last Movie** (**American Dreamer**, directed by Laurence Schiller), Hopper compares his work-in-progress to **The Magnificent Ambersons**. "I can become like Orson Welles – poor bastard", Hopper remarks, and then launches into a rant about Welles's inability to pry even $150,000 out of Universal[15].

Hopper's increasingly obsessive personal involvement in **The Last Movie** is reflected in the film's structure, where linear fictional story line gives way to the disintegration of cinematic representation. Moody, disconnected scenes make the story increasingly difficult to follow. The movie loses sync, the editing dissolves, the sound of the camera intrudes, the emulsion is scratched. Narrative becomes gesture, and the film gradually becomes a film about process and structure rather than character and plot. Most unsettling of all, perhaps, is the camera work, which becomes increasingly "artistic" as the film progresses. Under the influence of his cinematographer Laslo Kovaks, Hopper goes in for giant close-ups, leisurely focusing, ecstatic sunbursts, zooms, unusual camera angles, quick cuts, and strobe flash-forwards. Temporal and spatial unity collapse, quite against traditional audience expectations, and the film's structure is exposed by revealing to us the machinery of production, and by repeated references to the action going on behind the camera.

A MOVIE ABOUT CHAOS, OR A MOVIE ABOUT MOVIES?

When **The Last Movie** was first released, critics tended to regard it as an incoherent mess. Hopper was found guilty of committing "what the poet Yvor Winters called the imitative fallacy – the attempt to communicate a vision of chaos by creating a chaotic, disordered work of art (just as Antonioni is often accused of trying to portray the emptiness and boredom of modern society by producing empty and boring movies)"[16]. In recent years, however, particularly since the release of David Lynch's **Blue Velvet** (1986, which crystallized Hopper's almost mythic status in cinema history), **The Last Movie** has started to be reconsidered and revalued, mainly by a younger audience and a newer generation of critics. The recent video release cites a review from the *L.A. Times* which describes the film as "movie-making on the edge... impressive", and Hopper's "most ambitious, audacious work".

This new, more sympathetic generation of critics view **The Last Movie** as not merely a pastiche of self-contained narrative styles, but as a deliberate attempt to undercut our assumptions of narrative unity – in other words, an apocalyptic meta-film that questions the whole nature of narrative film-making. Today, **The Last Movie** tends to be regarded not as a movie about chaos, but as a movie about movies, parodying the illusions of popular culture, Hollywood westerns, cinematic naturalism and counter-cultural

Hopper with cinematographer, Laslo Kovaks

romanticism. Stuart Kaminsky, for example, describes **The Last Movie** as a "love-hate attack on contemporary movies, including [Hopper's] own, and our own assumptions about them"[17]. J. Hoberman describes the film as "absurd, delirious, confrontational... an act of visionary narcissism and an ode to failure"[18]. Richard Dorfman believes that the exile of the American film company in the movie serves as a metaphor for "the bankruptcy of their own myths which can no longer be promulgated in their own country, nor hold it together"[19]. And, according to William Siska, who devotes an entire chapter of his book *Modernism In The Narrative Cinema* to a reconsideration of **The Last Movie**:

"**The Last Movie** is not underground, but overground, not an independent film that eschews the traditions of the well-made film out of financial necessity, but a Hollywood-financed picture, shot in 35mm by a full consort of professionals, that rejects them by choice... The reflexive techniques used by Hopper in **The Last Movie** are used to discredit the validity of characters and actions within the narrative as 'real'. At the same time, they establish the 'reality' of the film itself[20]."

KANSAS AND KURTZ

The Last Movie is obviously influenced by a wide variety of previous films and earlier texts. In some cases, this influence is explicit; in other cases, less so. Connections with Fellini's **8½** seem self-evident; Hopper himself maintains that the light imagery in the movie was influenced by the Gnostic "Gospel According To St. Thomas", which was discovered in 1945 in a ruined temple near Nag Hamadi, Upper Egypt, and purports to be the sayings of Jesus as recorded by Didymos Judas Thomas[21]. The film also seems to be haunted by the specter of Charles Manson, by whom Hopper was fascinated. And then there are the many retrospective connections between Kansas and Marlon Brando's cruel and enigmatic Kurtz in Coppola's **Apocalypse Now**, vividly captured in the words of his agitated hippie disciple, a role also taken by Hopper, "The man is clear in his mind, but his soul is mad!".

Even more significant, however, is the influence on Hopper's Kansas of the original rendition of Kurtz, in Conrad's *Heart Of Darkness*. Like Conrad's Kurtz, the poncho-wearing Kansas also chooses to "go native" and stay behind in the wilderness long after his presence there is necessary, in order to obliquely exploit the wilds around him. Like Kurtz, Kansas is the inspiration for the growth of a bizarre cult; he appears to the "natives" in the guise of a "supernatural being... with the might of a deity" to whom they offer "unspeakable rites"[22]. In **The Last Movie**, these rites take the form of imitations of "American" behaviour. In the style of a cargo cult, the villagers begin shooting their own "movie", using wooden effigies of film cameras, and casting Kansas as their "star".

The final scene of the "movie fiesta", at which Kansas is ritually sacrificed, is connected in many ways to the procession of worship witnessed by Marlow in *Heart Of Darkness* that is dedicated to the dying Kurtz. In **The Last Movie**, the "movie fiesta" is vibrant and chaotic. Haunting Peruvian pipe music melds into the sound of Kris Kristofferson singing "Me And Bobby McGee", overlaid by ritual chanting and the clucking of chickens. The procession of Stetson-wearing villagers carries incense and candles along with animal masks, bones, guns and burning brands. Firecrackers are mounted on effigies of movie cameras and other wooden structures built to represent mikes, scaffolding and booms. One man plays the role of the director as the western shootout is reconstructed, with Kansas as its fatal hero-victim. This "movie-fiesta" provides the symbolic resolution to **The Last Movie**, as does the procession to worship Kurtz in *Heart Of Darkness*:

[T]hey shouted periodically together strings of amazing words that resembled no sounds of human language; and the deep murmurs of the crowd, interrupted suddenly, were like the responses of some Satanic litany... the wild crowd of obedient worshippers, the gloom of the forests, the glitter of the river between the murky bends, the beat of the drum regular and muffled like the beating of a heart, the heart of a conquering darkness.
It was a moment of triumph for the wilderness...

Unlike Kurtz, however, Kansas is a reluctant deity. He's terrified by the "unspeakable rites" that are offered up to him. Instead, he tries to show the villagers that they're wrong to believe so strongly in movies, that what happens in movies is "fake". Ultimately, the night before his death, after realizing that even the formerly critical Padre has joined "the movie church", he comes to regard cinema itself as a form of corruption ("we brought the movies", he cries to Maria; "that's where we made the mistake. We brought the movies..."). Unlike Kurtz, Kansas refuses to permit himself to be worshipped, and, as a result, is dragged through the streets like Christ on the Via Dolorosa, as the villagers drunkenly reconstruct the movie's final, fatal scenes.

The Kris Kristofferson song which recurs on the soundtrack at the end of **The Last Movie** includes the following lyrics:

"All of them princes, all of them gone,
All of them lovers in search of their own,
You can look to the mountains, and look to the sea
But don't you come crawling, 'cause you won't find me."

Kansas is sacrificed because he refuses to let the villagers worship him, refuses to let them "crawl" to him. Kurtz, on the other hand, is "crawled to", something which horrifies the narrator, Marlow, almost beyond words:

He was not afraid of the natives; they would not stir till Mr. Kurtz gave the word. His ascendency was extraordinary. The camps of these people surrounded the place, and the chiefs came every day to see him.
They would crawl... "I don't want to know anything of the ceremonies used when approaching Mr. Kurtz," I shouted. Curious, this feeling that came over me that such details would be more intolerable than the heads drying on the stakes under Mr. Kurtz's windows... The young man looked at me in surprise. I suppose it did not occur to him that Mr. Kurtz was no idol of mine... If it came to crawling before Kurtz, he crawled as much as the worst savage of them all.[23]

Like religion, movies give us something to believe in, something to distract us from our everyday reality, something to worship, something to "crawl to". For denouncing this belief in movies as a false one, Kansas is sacrificed with a shot to the chest. And as if to proclaim how very wrong his words are, the "fake" movie brings about a "real" death; the "camera" that "films" the sacrifice may be a fake one, but the bullets in the gun are for real.

NOTES

1. Reviews cit. in John Hoberman, *Dennis Hopper: From Method To Madness*, Minneapolis, MN: Walker Art Center, c.1988, p21.

2. Cit. in Ibid., p22.

3. Hoberman, p22.

4. Cit in Siska, William, *Modernism In The Narrative Cinema*, Arno Press, New York 1980: p80.

5. Darrach, Brad, "The Easy Rider In The Andes Runs Wild", *Life* (June 19, 1970), p49–59.

6. See Hoberman, p21.

7. Siska, p95.

8. Conner's films include **A Movie** (1958), **Cosmic Ray** (1961), **Vivian** (1964) **Report** (1964/5), and **For Mushrooms** (1960/66). They are typified by rapid cutting, collage, rhythm and juxtaposition.

9. Cit in Hoberman, p9.

10. Incidentally, Nicholas Ray, who directed Hopper in **Rebel**, reappears in a totemic role in Wim Wenders's 1977 movie **The American Friend**, also starring Hopper.

11. See, for example, Richard Combs, "The Last Movie", *Monthly Film Bulletin* vol. 49 #585 (October 1982), p219.

12. Hopper, Dennis, "How Far To The Last Movie?", *Monthly Film Bulletin* vol. 49 #585 (October 1982), p219.

13. Combs, p219.

14. Cit in Hoberman, p23, footnote 7.

15. Cit in Hoberman, p5.

16. Siska, p94.

17. Kaminsky, Stuart, "The Last Movie", *Take One*, vol. 3 #4 (March-April 1971), p30–31.

18. Hoberman, p20.

19. Dorfman, Richard, "Fathers And Sons", *The Velvet Light Trap* 14 (Winter 1975), pp 42-44.

20. Siska, pp 81, 98.

21. See Hoberman, p16.

22. Conrad, Joseph, *Heart Of Darkness*, ed. Robert Kimbaugh, Norton Critical Edition, NY and London 1988: p50.

23. Conrad, p58.

'TRACKS': DENNIS HOPPER'S JOURNEY TO VIETNAM AND BACK

Vietnam was the first TV war. Images of the conflict were fed nightly to the folks at home, with inevitably devastating results. While every previous war had been witnessed from a safe distance, Nam was pumped directly to America, uncensored. Every atrocity, every failure, every mistake and every casualty was brought home with a reality and immediacy that cut through all the flag waving and made people wonder about just what was happening. It's unsurprising that in every war since, the authorities have sought to restrict television images of bloody, broken bodies, instead encouraging computer game-style thermal imaging of bombs striking distant targets, and reinvesting the slaughter of civilians as "collateral damage". Vietnam also spawned a unique movie genre. Previously, war films tended to show the conflicts as glorious crusades, with clean cut All-American heroes fighting for what was right. The trauma of Nam, for both veterans and the nation as a whole, changed all that for years; it was only when Reagan became President, and encouraged America to once again see war as a macho game, that Nam could become a playground for action men like Sly Stallone.

During the Seventies, movies about Vietnam tended to fall into two distinct groups. Films which dealt with the conflict itself were relatively few – **The Deer Hunter, Apocalypse Now**, and the little known but devastating **Physical Assault** are among the prime examples. The larger group of films dealt with consequences – mentally fucked-up kids who returned home from the war, unable to readjust to normal life. Vietnam Vets became synonymous with mental instability. When a gunman went berserk in a movie, you could be sure that he was a Vet. When a serial killer started to kill off women, it was almost certain that he would be plagued by Nam flashbacks. Bizarre films like **Cannibal Apocalypse** even suggested that the trauma of Vietnam would result in an insatiable craving for human flesh.

Falling in between these two groups is Henry Jaglom's **Tracks** – a quiet, thoughtful movie (with psychotic interludes) which plays like the missing link between **How Sleep The Brave** and **Coming Home**, and which fills in the plot holes which prevented **The Deer Hunter** from working. **Tracks** also stars Dennis Hopper, giving arguably the finest performance of his career – a career which has been consistently coloured by the Vietnam war, either directly or indirectly. While **Tracks** and **Apocalypse Now** are clearly *about* the war, Nam has infiltrated many of Hopper's films. In **Texas Chainsaw Massacre 2**, he not only squares up against the ultimate Nam casualty psycho ("Choptop"), but also seems like a crazed vet himself as the movie progresses; in **Easy Rider** and **The Trip**, Hopper was the face of the anti-war movement, and when he's gunned down at the end of **Easy Rider**, the parallels with the Vietnam wars (both the conflict in Asia and the conflict between generations of American people) are only too obvious. Even a film like **Colors**, directed by Hopper in 1988, seems to be influenced and tainted by memories of Nam, with the ghettos of Los Angeles standing in for the killing fields of Vietnam.

Tracks is unusual because it is so clearly about Vietnam, yet takes place entirely within the American heartland, on one of those endless cross-country rail journeys that seem so alien to British viewers, who can complete even the longest trip in a single day. It also seems alien to see counter-culture rebel Hopper in full military uniform, looking almost cartoonly smart. As the radio announcement at the film's opening tells us, the war is finally over – Hopper is coming home. But the radio is wrong – Hopper's war, like the internal wars of so many Vietnam vets, is far from over. It still rages inside him – a fact we almost take for granted after years of maladjusted Vets in countless movies from **Taxi Driver** to **Combat Shock**; more significantly though, Hopper is still on duty. His war doesn't end until he's delivered a coffin carrying the body of one of his buddies to his home town for burial where, Hopper constantly tells his fellow passengers, "he's gonna have a band, he's gonna have a parade". We never believe such optimism – again, there is too much history, too many scenes of Vietnam vets skulking home, the losing army in a war which no-one wanted, for us to expect a hero's welcome for Hopper and his charge.

    Tracks opens with a shot of Hopper addressing an unseen passenger. "Do you think about your childhood often?" he asks. "I think about mine when the going gets rough." By the end of his question, Hopper is looking directly at the camera, directly at us. He's laying out the whole central theme of the film right there. Traumatised by the present, Hopper is constantly reverting to the past. Throughout the film, he clings to ideas of a childhood which was somehow safer and easier (as all childhoods are); he listens to Forties dance tunes, morale-boosting recording from an earlier war which was only seen from the safety of Hollywood movies, in black and white. When we think of the Second World War, we see it in monochrome – a bloodless, distant event. When we think of Nam, we see grainy, hand-held newsreel footage in lurid colours, napalmed children and dangerous, drug-addled US troops out of control.

    Vietnam was the only war where the public saw reality. Earlier conflicts were distanced by time and technology, while later conflicts like the Gulf war were carefully stage-managed by Governments who knew only too well the impact of burning bodies on television viewers. Nam was there in all its glory, beamed uncensored into living rooms across America and the world

every night. So we can all relate to Hopper's retreat into a "safe" world (no matter that World War Two was even bloodier than Vietnam in reality).

Hopper's three day journey home is, in reality, his journey back to reality from the madness of war, and it's not an easy one. He wanders the length of the train (and again – for the sake of rail travellers in the UK – this train has spacious restaurant cars, bars, cabins etc) in search of human contact. He flits from passenger to passenger, trying to start or join conversations, but he doesn't know how to. He can't fit in. In his stiff, straight uniform, Hopper looks like an anomaly; even when he changes into street clothes, he still seems woefully out of place. Much of this is thanks to Hopper's wonderful performance – a twitchy, sweaty performance that initially makes us feel sorry for him, embarrassed for him as he nervously attempts to rejoin society.

Much of the dialogue in **Tracks** feels improvised, and the film has a documentary feel to it, using hand-held cameras and observational techniques. We catch snippets of empty conversation – talk about sex, chess, business, etc. The talk of normality. The film has an almost documentary feel during these early scenes, its deliberate banality making it more real than any stage-managed fly-on-the-wall docu-soap. The film presents a false sense of boredom – false because the viewer is never bored, yet feels as though nothing is happening. And in many ways, for the first thirty minutes of the film, nothing *is* – yet in many ways, *everything* important takes place in this

opening section. We meet Hopper and his fellow passengers, we learn about his final mission with the coffin, and we experience his sense of alienation. But unlike many films which hammer such points home to the viewer, **Tracks** presents them so subtly that we are barely aware of them. Only as the film progresses do they become important.

Tracks moves forward when Hopper and fellow passenger Dean Stockwell put the moves on a couple of girls who have joined the train. Hopper and Stockwell are an interesting mix – Hopper the shy man in uniform, Stockwell the hairy, brightly dressed easy rider. While Stockwell schmoozes his way to romantic success, Hopper is way out of his depth. He tells pretty hippie girl Stephanie (Taryn Power) "I haven't seen anything like you since I was sixteen. I'm not even sure that I saw it then." She's sufficiently interested in him to go back to his room, despite his painfully clumsy chat-up techniques, but when he comes on too strong ("let me show you how I like to kiss," she tells him after an over-enthusiastic petting session), she leaves. Hopper's desperation (for love? For connection?) has driven her away, and he starts to lose it. Slowly. The next morning, Hopper has a brief fling with an older female passenger after asking for shampoo (she washes his hair before surrendering to some intense, passionate and very real foreplay), but he still wants to connect with Power. Meanwhile, his lack of connection to everyone else is becoming more obvious. Things reach a

head when Hopper is again talking about his mission. "Why do you feel you have a monopoly on feeling sorry for yourself?" asks a black Korean war veteran as Hopper explains to him that he's escorting a coffin "with a black man in it". The Korean vet is unimpressed. "You only have one, I had twenty-one," he comments. But Hopper is no longer listening. Hopper is instead watching as Power is harassed by another passenger, who then starts to assault her. Other passengers join in what soon becomes a gang-rape, and Hopper pulls his gun. Of course, none of this has actually happened. It's a hallucination, the first sign that Hopper's trip is rapidly becoming a bad one. Two days into the journey, fifty minutes into the film, and Hopper's sense of alienation gives way to mental instability.

This hallucination represents a turning point in the film, much as Max Renn's visions do in David Cronenberg's **Videodrome**. From this point onwards, we cannot trust what we see. We wonder how much is reality, and how much is false... and we begin to question what has already gone.

There is also an air of unreality about Hopper's quaintly touching relationship with Power. It's an oddly affecting, though clearly doomed affair that is old fashioned in its romance. Power seems somehow out of time; even more so as we watch the film today, her hippie look seeming almost as dated as the Glen Miller that Hopper listens to as they dance, in the final moment of lucid normality. After this touching interlude, it all comes crumbling down for Hopper.

When MP's board the train, Hopper flips – he stashes his uniform in the toilet and runs naked through the train (a nude scene which still seems startling today, given the lack of male nudity in mainstream cinema) as he seeks to escape those who are hunting him. Only it's not Hopper they want. Stockwell bursts into his cabin and reveals himself as a political radical war protester. This revelation does little for Hopper, who rejects his pleas for help. Stockwell, whose free speech is too much for the powers that be in the land of the free, is captured and taken away. The pushy real estate salesman who has been pushing land deals throughout the film is revealed as a part-time government agent. Does this feel real?

Genuine or not, Hopper's obvious hallucinations get worse. "They *know* what you've done," sneers a waiter at one point. Fellow passengers warn him of impending danger. They deny knowledge of each other. Nothing feels right. Nothing feels real.

Hopper and Power take a day out of their journey to make love in a field – Power giving Hopper the "one nice thing" that his life is missing. It's an idyllic scene – there's no sound but the wind blowing. But mid-sex, Hopper loses control. He confesses to rejecting Stockwell's pleas for help, claiming that it was impossible for him to do otherwise – "I'm on a very important mission. Guys like that have to be sacrificed". Peacenik Power is repulsed, and flees. Hopper is finally alone. No lovers. No passengers. Just him and the coffin.

When Hopper reaches the end of the line (and doesn't that suddenly sound symbolic?), there is – surprise surprise – no welcoming committee. No parade, no band. Just a couple of embarrassed looking officials to handle the funeral. Biding his time until the burial, Hopper wanders around town, even more out of place. Anonymous. Forgotten. He reverts to childhood again – visiting school rooms, an empty home. And there's the realisation. Hopper is supposedly returning his dead comrade home, but it's *him* who has returned to his home town. This is Hopper's old school, Hopper's old home, to a town that doesn't care what has happened to him, where people will come out with glib comments like "I wish I could've been there", not knowing that everyone who was in Vietnam wanted to be anywhere but there. Hopper is back in his spiritual home, and he's brought Vietnam – his mental home – with him.

It's never good to reveal the ending of a movie. It spoils the surprise – and it's only an unexpected ending that is worth revealing – for anyone who hasn't seen the film, even when, as is the case here, that ending is the best known part of the whole production. But sometimes it has to be done. **Tracks** virgins beware: I'm about to reveal the ending.

Tracks ends in the cemetery. Hopper stands over the coffin, alongside the dutiful, embarrassed looking officials. "He's the biggest hero that's ever been here. No-one showed up," muses Hopper *(Hopper's the biggest hero that's ever been there. No-one showed up).* As the flag-draped coffin is lowered into the ground, Hopper demands a moment alone. The embarrassed-looking officials leave and Hopper gazes into the grave. And finally cracks completely.

It's one of cinema's most powerful moments – a tour-de-force of acting[1], writing and controlled direction which, even seen out of context, packs a hell of a punch; within the context of **Tracks**, Hopper's final, incoherent yet revelatory monologue is what finally confirms this film as one of the finest movies to emerge in the post-**Easy Rider** era of American independent cinema[2].

Hopper moans: "I love... I love... I really love... I really do love... I love, I love and I hate, and I hate, and I hate, because I love... because I love I hate, because I love I hate, because I love I hate, because I love, because I love... YOU MOTHERFUCKERS!"

Hopper jumps into the grave, opens up the coffin and reveals the secret which we suddenly realise we knew all along. There is no dead buddy, no hero, no great black man. The dead man is Hopper, a small town boy who went to war and lost his mind. And now he's home. "You wanna go to Nam?" he screams; "I'll take you to Nam. I'll take you there!"

Hopper unwraps the tarpaulin, puts on the combat helmet and tools up with the guns'n'ammo that the coffin contains. Then he leaps out of the grave, ready to take the whole town to Nam...

NOTES

1. Hopper's amazing portrayal of mental disintegration and eventual psychosis here achieves the raw truth he would evince in later roles such as Donny in **Out Of The Blue**, Frank in **Blue Velvet**, and the eponymous **Paris Trout**. These are remorseless characterizations which seem to emanate from a place beyond "acting", the place that Hopper himself has alluded to as an automatic zone of "total recall".

2. And indeed the film was only made possible by **Easy Rider**'s success, which led to a string of further productions from its producers Raybert, who re-organized as BBS under the direction of Bob Rafelson, Steve Blaunter and Bert Schneider. BBS folded in 1973 after making such movies as **Five Easy Pieces** (1970), the Jack Nicholson-directed **Drive, He Said** (1971) and Henry Jaglom's **A Safe Place** (1971); but the Hollywood mould was broken, and Jaglom and Schneider were reunited for **Tracks**.

'THE AMERICAN FRIEND'

The late seventies were, on the whole, not kind to Dennis Hopper. A few years previously he'd still been able to bring his quivering paranoiac sensibilities to underrated, little-seen gems such as **Tracks** (1976) and **Mad Dog Morgan** (Philippe Mora, 1976), but now he was reduced to plying his trade in such Euro-obscurities as **Les Apprentis Sorciers** (1977) and **L'Ordre Et La Sécurité Du Monde** (1978).

In the middle of this period, however, he starred in a curious German film, **Der Amerikanische Freund/The American Friend** (1977), directed by highly respected arthouse director Wim Wenders. The director had always been concerned with the relationship between the new and old world, and more specifically America's cultural influence on post-war Germany – after all, he was best known at the time for adapting for the continent the quintessentially American concept of the road movie, with his **Im Lauf Der Zeit/Kings Of The Road** (1976). Here he set out to explore this relationship in a thriller format, adapting Patricia Highsmith's novel *Ripley's Game*, third in a series dealing with the misadventures of an amoral, chameleon-like anti-hero – Mersault with more criminal acumen.

Based rather loosely at times on the source novel, the film is ultimately, like the Ripley novels before it, not much of a thriller at all. There is no clear-cut distinction between heroes and villains, little sense of resolution and only a handful of scenes dedicated to building up suspense. It tells the story of Jonathan Zimmermann (Bruno Ganz), a picture framer in Hamburg who suffers from an untreatable blood disease and is tricked into believing his condition to be worse than it actually is by Tom Ripley (Hopper), an American art dealer specialising in forgeries. This is done as a favour by Ripley to his associate Raoul Minot, who then approaches Zimmermann and offers him a substantial sum of money to commit one or two murders. While Zimmermann is initially shocked, he comes to believe that he has little to lose and much to gain, Minot playing on his fear that he will leave no money to his wife and son. Zimmermann commits the first murder and then, albeit reluctantly, acquiesces to one more on a train. Ripley is horrified by the idea of a second murder, and ends up helping Zimmermann on the train with, ultimately, devastating effects for all involved.

1. *"What's wrong with a cowboy in Hamburg?"*
    —Tom Ripley, *The American Friend*.

Patricia Highsmith didn't like the adaptation of her novel. *The American Friend* not only mixes in, in typically Hollywood style, many elements from the second Ripley novel, *Ripley Under Ground*, and relocates the action from

France to Germany, but also makes substantial changes to the character of Ripley. The differences are instructive. While in the Ripley novels Tom Ripley has embraced a European identity as firmly as most US immigrants embrace the idea of America, in the film Ripley is very much an American. He wears a cowboy hat almost everywhere he goes, drives a large American car, lives in an ostentatiously opulent mansion with a pool table and a Wurlitzer jukebox in the basement, and speaks German only very, very badly.

By contrast the Ripley of the novels is a chameleon, a fluent linguist, blending effortlessly into the background of whatever situation he finds himself in. After the beginning of the first novel we never again see him in the USA, while Hopper's Ripley is constantly travelling back and forth between New York and Hamburg. Highsmith's Ripley is a married man – Hopper's is a loner. In the novels, moreover, although he eventually seems content with his ostensibly reputable situation in France, he enjoys role-playing – in the first novel, in most of which he assumes the identity of a man he has killed, he enjoys it to an almost pathological degree. Assuming the identity of a dead man is the end of the line, the most desperate act in film noir terms – see Edgar Ulmer's **Detour** (1945) – and there is the sense in films featuring such characters that they have lost any moral sense, adrift in a vacuum. Contemporary reviews of the first novel in the series, *The Talented Mr Ripley*, refer to the eponymous protagonist as "a schizophrenic murderer" – in, one assumes, the popular sense of a split personality – and passages such as the following show why:

He went up to Dickie's room and paced around for a few moments, his hands in his pockets. He wondered when Dickie was coming back? Or was he going to stay and make an afternoon of it, really take her to bed with him? He jerked Dickie's closet door open and looked in. There was a freshly pressed, new-looking grey flannel suit that he had never seen Dickie wearing. Tom took it out. He took off his knee-length shorts and put on the grey flannel trousers. He put on a pair of Dickie's shoes. Then he opened the bottom drawer of the chest and took out a clean blue-and-white striped shirt.

He chose a dark-blue silk tie and knotted it carefully. The suit fitted him. He re-parted his hair and put the part a little more to one side, the way Dickie wore his.

"Marge, you must understand that I don't love you," Tom said into the mirror in Dickie's voice, with Dickie's higher pitch on the emphasised words, with the little growl in the throat at the end of the phrase that could be pleasant or unpleasant, intimate or cool, according to Dickie's mood. "Marge, stop it!" Tom turned suddenly and made a grab in the air as if he were seizing Marge's throat. He shook her, twisted her, while she sank lower and lower, until at last he left her, limp, on the floor. He was panting. He wiped his forehead the way Dickie did, reached for a handkerchief and, not finding any, got one from Dickie's top drawer, then resumed in front of the mirror. Even his parted lips looked like Dickie's lips when he was out of breath from swimming, drawn down a little from his lower teeth. "You know why I had to do that," he said, still breathlessly, addressing Marge, though he watched himself in the mirror. "You were interfering between Tom and me – No, not that! But there is a bond between us!"

(—*The Talented Mr Ripley*, Patricia Highsmith)

Although Hopper's Ripley expresses some confusion about his identity, stating early on into his Dictaphone that "I know less and less about who I am – or who anyone else is", in his actions and appearance throughout the film he has a consistent and coherent identity – he is an American. What identity confusion there is might be seen as representing the fracture inherent in being American, reflecting the contradictions of such an identity – but it is throughout far better defined and less amorphous than is the identity of Highsmith's Ripley. This emphasis and insistence on Ripley's American identity, even to the point of referring to it in the title of the film, reflects Wenders' desire to make more of the film than a "mere" thriller, and to introduce and explore themes entirely missing from the Ripley novels themselves – principally those of American cultural dominance and the influence of American film, to which we'll return later.

Now Wenders actually works in Hollywood itself, directing misbegotten pap like **The End Of Violence** (1997), and has virtually disowned all of his earlier work. **Paris, Texas** (1984) and **Wings Of Desire** (1987) are his most famous and popular films, both dealing with the marketable themes of love, companionship and resolution; but the ambiguous, opaque meanderings of **The American Friend** represent, to my mind, his finest work.

2.   *"I can fake a Picasso as well as anyone else"*
                    —Picasso, as reported in **F For Fake** (Orson Welles, 1974)

Notions of authenticity are key to the film. The plot depends upon Zimmermann believing a series of forged medical reports, and Ripley only chooses to trick him because Zimmermann correctly casts doubt on the authenticity of one of Ripley's paintings. The forgeries, explored at length in *Ripley Under Ground*, seem to be how Ripley makes his money. He buys them from a painter in NYC who is imitating the style of a dead painter called "Derwatt", then sells them to collectors in Europe. At an auction Zimmermann warns an American colleague, Allan Winter, not to bid for one of Ripley's Derwatts as its seems to have been faked, but Winter is keen nonetheless, knowing that he will be able to sell it in the USA. Zimmermann seems alone in the film in caring about truth and authenticity, but is then inconsistent and hypocritical, lying to his wife about the murders he commits. Within the mechanics of the film, Zimmermann's lying to his wife seems actually far more important in a moral appraisal of the character than do the murders themselves.

Notions of authenticity and truth are moreover fluid within the film, and for Zimmermann a previously certain world (if one involving the threat of death) becomes one characterised by uncertainty and ambiguity. Although it is clear to the viewer that some of Zimmermann's medical reports are faked, at the end of the film he dies. The implication is that he has weakened himself through overaction and stress throughout the film – we see him being explicitly warned by his doctor not to overexert himself – and this worsens his

condition, leading to his death. We see the effects of his illness – immediately before the first murder, he begins to stumble and cuts his head, and elsewhere suffers severe dizzy spells – and are aware of the physical trials he is put through, such as guarding Ripley's mansion in the cold, while Ripley blithely plays with the jukebox inside. The medical reports were faked, but in their prediction of Zimmermann's impending death, surely their key message, they are correct. There are a number of other indications in the film that the dichotomy between authentic/fake, between true/false, is a flawed, perhaps untenable division.

Ambiguity also characterises our view of the two central characters, Ripley and Zimmermann, whose peculiar relationship recalls to a degree that of Turner and Chas in Donald Cammell's **Performance** (1968). Zimmermann is a highly moral family man involved in the low-key but respectable business of picture framing – but he kills a number of men. Ripley is clearly involved in a number of criminal ventures and sets Zimmermann up for the events of the film, but also helps him, saving his life on the train. There is ultimately no "good guy"/"bad guy" dichotomy here; both are fallible, human – Hopper's performance is a world away from the psychotics he is best known for – and through their friendship they become ever more similar to each other, both admitting hitherto unexplored sides to their personalities.

The ideas of art forgery and ambiguous authenticity recall the work of an American iconoclast whose career, incidentally, shows at times bizarre similarities to that of Hopper – Orson Welles. In 1973 Welles saw a half-hour documentary made for French TV by François Reichenbach on the art forger Elmyr de Hory. Taken with the idea of expanding the piece into a full-length feature, he bought the complete footage of the film, including outtakes, and developed it into a feature, **F For Fake**, a lengthy meditation "about trickery, about fraud, about – lies." The film, while being entirely enjoyable on its own merits, sheds light on a number of the key themes in *The American Friend*.

The principal focus of the film is on two forgers – one, Elmyr de Hory, the most celebrated art forger of the century, and the other, Clifford Irving, who wrote a book about de Hory as well as his own fake biography of Howard Hughes. The film is playful and elliptical, recounting endless tales of fakery – Howard Hughes was reputed to have used a double, and some speculated that Irving's fake biography was narrated to him by Hughes' double, playing a trick on Hughes; Welles' own tale of the radio broadcast of *The War Of The Worlds*, which brought the nation to a state of absolute panic; again and again Welles explores the idea of the "fake" affecting the "real". In the art world, "the genuine quality of a painting isn't so much whether it's a real painting or a fake – it's whether it's a good fake or a bad fake", and art critics are shown to be entirely fallible, dealers unperturbed by fakes – so long as they make money. There are intimations, however, that the confusion between the two can be more problematic – as in the broadcast of *The War Of The Worlds*.

Fictions are constructed within labyrinthine fictions, but there is one theme Welles returns to again and again – that of film. *F For Fake* utilises the framing device of having Welles in an editing suite, watching, occasionally rewinding and commenting on the footage. Film itself is the greatest fakery – as Welles states, "I am a charlatan". But film is a form of fakery which has an enormous impact on the viewer's perception of "reality". It's interesting that James Ferman, formerly president of the BBFC, should have written, in passing the film for the Board, that "F For Fake has impressed us more than any film ever submitted to the Board". Or maybe this document itself was faked?

3.   *"I brought you something – a gift"*
        —Tom Ripley to Jonathan Zimmermann, **The American Friend**.

Optical toys, precursors to the cinema, appear time and again: Zimmermann gives Ripley one the first time the latter walks into his shop, apologising for the minor rudeness which leads Ripley to involve him in the first place; Ripley later gives Zimmermann a similar object as a gift; Zimmermann's son is seen playing with a zoetrope; and the train victims are overheard discussing film as they board the train – we overhear references to "fifty to seventy-five prints" and a "German co-production." These are not merely incidental details, but point to a larger concern within the film.

Wenders cast Nicholas Ray as the art forger and Sam Fuller as the leader of those killed on the train in **The American Friend** – two classic American directors, whose emphasis on modern, especially mainstream cinema cannot be over-emphasised. Nicholas Ray directed **Rebel Without A Cause** (1955), featuring a young Dennis Hopper, and Hopper had cast Fuller in **The Last Movie** (1971)[1]. Wenders himself also appears in the film, wrapped in bandages in a fake ambulance. The casting of these characters is important – Ray, especially, as a forger – and underlines Wenders' desire to use the film partly as a metaphor for the relationship between the USA and post-war Germany – a relationship characterised, as with the USA and most European countries, by cultural domination, principally through the medium of film. That the intimations are subtle, the argument implicit, is perhaps not so much reflective of deliberate opacity on the part of Wenders as it is an indication of how far this influence goes, how all-pervasive it is – we simply don't notice it any more.

It's worth asking in this context why Wenders cast Hopper in the role of Ripley. Hopper wasn't much of a popular star at the time, and the only major American film he appeared in during the '70s was **Apocalypse Now** (1979), completed two years after **The American Friend** – although Hopper there looks about fifteen years older, the ravages of endemic substance use finally having caught up with him. Nothing in Hopper's CV of cowboys, hippies and psychotics would lead one on the surface to suspect that he could play Tom Ripley for Wenders, but his is an extremely effective portrayal.

In fact it's precisely this back catalogue which makes Hopper so perfect in the role. His early screen appearances are those of the quintessential American in rugged individualist mode: the troubled '50s teenager (**Rebel Without A Cause, Giant** – it's worth noting that Hopper twice played alongside James Dean, one of the ultimate American screen icons), the cowboy (**From Hell To Texas, True Grit**), the biker (**The Glory Stompers**) and the hippy (**The Trip, Easy Rider**).

All are a part of the American ethos, and as such Hopper can be seen as representing this, but even in some of the earlier movies – and certainly by the time of **The Last Movie** – he was displaying a dislocated quality, a sense of fracture which he has since exploited for his many overwrought psychotics – even icons have to pay the bills. The combination of being quintessentially American and borderline psychotic is perfect for **The American Friend**. It's also worth noting that **The Last Movie**, Hopper's directorial masterpiece, deals, in a far more explicit and exclusive way than **The American Friend**,

with one of the same themes – the influence of Americana (with an emphasis on film) on a foreign culture.

The section of **The American Friend** in which Zimmermann is taken to Paris by Minot, undergoing a medical test for which the results are faked then committing his first murder, has an unreal quality. There is the sense almost of the murder sequence being from a different film – it is an exercise in suspense, a tense period in what might be considered a slow film – filmic, perhaps, in an otherwise literary film. We don't know how many American films Zimmermann watches – Wenders avoids giving crassly obvious pointers – and the only time we see him with a TV, it gives him an electric shock when he tries to turn it on. His only concession to pop culture is his incessant humming of Beatles tunes. But there are a number of subtle indications of the influence of film – the clichéd screen villain look of Minot's Parisian associate, who points Zimmermann's first victim out to him; Zimmermann's performance throughout the first Paris sequence, that of someone acting out a role with which he is only familiar through films; and an important scene in which he, having arrived in Charles de Gaulle airport, sees a man collapse at the top of an escalator. The image clearly stays in his mind, as he recreates it when killing his first victim on the Paris metro escalator – the implication being that the action duplicates the image.

Wenders here is not, I feel, trying to comment on film violence – which seems, incidentally, the only negative effect of film that censors and indeed Wenders himself nowadays (cf **The End Of Violence**) consider important – but rather about the imposition of American cultural values, perhaps principally through film. One can see this film then as an extended metaphor on the relationship between America, with Hollywood as its great propaganda machine, and post-war Germany.

To see the metaphor as representing merely the corruption of German culture by a rapacious Hollywood is to oversimplify it. In the film Zimmermann is diseased from the outset, and acquiesces perhaps too readily in the demands made of him to commit a number of murders. Conversely, Ripley clearly regrets having involved him in this situation, and eventually helps and befriends him. The metaphor is further complicated by the fact that this is, after all, a film. Not only does it star American film directors in a number of key roles, but it also features Ganz and Hopper, both important stars in their countries of origin, and both to a degree representing the film industries of their respective countries – Ganz principally noted for starring in cerebral works by Wenders and Werner Herzog, while Hopper is an old hand in exploitation movies. While **The American Friend** lacks the formal deconstructive elements of, say, Godard's movies in its exploration of the relationship between film and "reality", it remains an extended meditation on this, among other themes, succeeding both despite and because of its unresolved ambiguities.

Where are they now? Hopper is, ironically enough, an art collector and painter himself, and hasn't starred in a truly great movie since David Lynch's **Blue Velvet** (1986). Wenders is, as has previously been noted, currently making the worst films of his career, and is concerned with an altogether more obvious debate on the nature of film. Typically, of the four Ripley novels, it is the two which have already been filmed which are currently being remade (apart from **The American Friend**, the first Ripley novel was filmed previously as **Plein Soleil** [aka **Purple Noon**, René Clement, 1959], a French film bearing marked similarities, again, to **F For Fake**). Going on previous experience, these new Hollywood efforts seem most likely to be thin shadows – bad forgeries – of the original films. In the new version of **The American Friend** I expect Zimmermann to be cured of his blood disease at the end. You saw it here first.

NOTES

1. Fuller – director of such pulp classics as **Shock Corridor** (1963) and **The Naked Kiss** (1964) – also appeared in Wenders' **The End Of Violence**, shortly before his death. And in 1980 Wenders had co-directed **Lightning Over Water** with Nicholas Ray, shot over the last few weeks of Ray's life.

'OUT OF THE BLUE'

A poisonous punk gesture of almost unparalleled "fuck you" potential, Dennis Hopper's apocalyptic **Out Of The Blue** is not a film to take lightly in its unflinching and disturbing portrait of a deeply dysfunctional family mired in incest and abuse. That Hopper also plays the vile protagonist of this exercise in shock treatment makes it a fascinating psychological portrait of the man in his darkest days.

Out Of The Blue is also arguably the pivotal film in the canon of '80s U.S. punk movies – a genre that also includes Penelope Spheeris' **Suburbia** (1983) and **The Decline Of The Western Civilisation Part One** (1980), Abel Ferrara's **Driller Killer** (1979) and Alex Cox's **Repo Man** (1984) – films that pushed well beyond the boundaries of public acceptance in documenting the lives of America's disenfranchised youth.

The film follows the exploits of CeeBee, a 15-year-old delinquent tom-boy who dreams of being a rock star. She lives with Kathy, her junkie mother, and is waiting for Donny, her father, to return from prison to re-unite their family. He has been serving a five year manslaughter sentence for his part in an accident that wiped out a bus full of school kids. We see a 10-year-old CeeBee, dressed as a clown in the cab of her father's truck. More concerned with drinking and flirting with his daughter than watching the road, Don rams straight into the bus, which has stalled across both lanes. Children's screams mesh with screeching tires and rending metal.

Cut to 15-year-old CeeBee shaking off this nightmare vision, and going out to the cab, which now sits unused and overgrown with weeds in front of the house. She switches on the CB radio and recites Situationist punk slogans to bemused truckers – "Disco sucks. Kill all hippies. Subvert Normality. Punk is not sexual, it's just aggression."

CeeBee has a fixation with Elvis and Sid Vicious, and expresses her desire to kill herself because following their deaths "life is meaningless". She spends her spare time smashing drums and raising tuneless hell with a guitar, like her punk idols. Kathy takes her to prison to see Donny, who becomes emotional at seeing his daughter for the first time in five years.

After an argument with Kathy, CeeBee hitch-hikes to the big city, where she takes in the strange sights and is befriended by a cab driver, who takes her home to get high but then tries to rape her. CeeBee smashes a bottle over his head, flees and finds herself in a punk club with a show in full swing. She makes her way backstage and hangs out with the group's drummer, who fulfils her dream by letting her play drums during the encore.

Returning home, CeeBee and Kathy visit a child psychologist, who threatens to take CeeBee into care to combat her continuing truancy. Kathy cites Donny's imminent homecoming as the solution to their problems, but

OUT OF BLUE

things don't work out so smoothly. Donny's homecoming party is broken up by the arrival of Anderson, the father of one of the children who died in the crash, who threatens to make Donny's life difficult. On family outings, it becomes obvious that Donny's relationship to his daughter is stronger than the one he has with his wife. Anderson gets Donny fired from his job, but before leaving, he steals some sticks of dynamite.

Donny and his best friend Charlie, who has become Kathy's drug buddy and surrogate lover in Donny's absence, plan their revenge on Anderson. They cosh him outside the bowling alley he owns, steal a briefcase full of money and celebrate with a night of wild partying, during which time Donny's dark side emerges. He decides that Charlie should fuck CeeBee "to stop her becoming a dyke". But CeeBee has overheard them and is preparing to defend herself. The situation triggers her memory of the sexual abuse Donny inflicted on her as a child, a fact she forces him to confront before stabbing him to death. She then takes Kathy out to the truck, lights the fuse of the dynamite and blows up what's left of her contaminated nuclear family to smithereens.

In Linda Manz (who plays CeeBee), Hopper found an archetypal punk heroine – young, androgynous, assured and aggressive. Manz had previously appeared as a child actor in **The Wanderers** (1979) and Terrence Malick's **Days Of Heaven** (1978), and has been seen more recently in Harmony Korine's **Gummo** and the Michael Douglas vehicle **The Game**. But for anyone that has seen **Out Of The Blue**, Manz is unforgettable as the street-wise adolescent whose innocence has been brutalised and battle-scarred.

Early in the movie, CeeBee asks her mother which parent she most resembles. She replies that CeeBee is "kinda tough and sexy" like her father, "except a girl". CeeBee's reaction is telling. "A girl Don," she says, laughing at the description of herself, but that is exactly what she is. In her father's absence, she has taken on his attributes, even assuming the dominant role in her relationship with her mother.

Hopper claimed that **Out Of The Blue** hit a raw nerve with its depiction of "the society of North America" where "the family unit is falling apart". But in a very real sense, the impact of the film is equally due to its depiction of Dennis Hopper falling apart. And perhaps it's fitting that a film about such horrific abuse and self-destruction was made by a man who, over the years, has proved himself a master at it.

In 1979, Hopper spent time in the Philippines for his role as photo-journalist Hurley in **Apocalypse Now** (a by-word for Hollywood excess), which may suggest the kind of mental state he was in by the time he came to make **Out Of The Blue** a year later. In the intervening period, he went home to Taos, New Mexico. It was meant to be downtime, but Hopper ended up making another movie, **Human Highway** (Dean Stockwell, 1982), and getting fucked up for months on end in bars with his friend Neil Young (the film's star and producer) while scouting locations. (After shooting, Hopper was sued by actress Sally Kirkland, who alleged that he severed a tendon on her index finger with a knife during a violent outburst.[1]) It has to be said that, as Donny, Hopper looks as if he's in a psychotic state. In virtually every scene he's clutching a drink or a bottle, supping on whiskey as if it was mother's milk. His slate-gray hair is brushed forward, unkempt and greasy. His face is gaunt and eyes glazed like a perpetual drunk. It's an anti-image that haunts his early '80s movies, the period Hopper was reportedly almost totally out of control and at his most rip-roaringly self-destructive.

At Donny's homecoming party, he stumbles and struts around the room like a sozzled Rod Stewart, dancing with Charlie, reciting a litany of illegal substances – coke, smack, speed – he jealously assumes his best friend has been abusing in his absence. When Anderson, the father of one of the kids who died in the crash comes to confront Donny later that night, he tries to diffuse the situation with drink. "Look, I'm an asshole," Donny says, pouring a bottle of Scotch over his head. "But I'm not a motherfuckin', *dumb* asshole," he holds the bottle upright again, "because there's enough here for

two drinks." Anderson just looks at Donny disgustedly and walks out, despite the pleas of his friends to "bust some heads".

While Billy, Hopper's character in **Easy Rider**, got stoned on the open road in a search for identity, Donny gets stoned to wipe his out. He's found out what and who he is and he doesn't like what he sees. The alcohol breaks down his psyche's protective barriers, releasing his inner demons and forcing his family to confront them. In "Dennis Hopper: Out Of The Blue & Into The Black"[2], Adrian Martin sees Hopper's '80s persona (and specifically his role as actor/director of **Out Of The Blue**) as an embodiment of the hippie "dream gone bad" and that, in cultural terms, the actor represents "a foul truth risen to the surface".

Henry D. Herring's essay "Out Of The Dream And Into The Nightmare: Dennis Hopper's Apocalyptic Vision Of America"[3] contrasts the sepia-toned soul-searching of **Easy Rider** with the garish, aggressive nihilism of **Out Of The Blue**. He suggests that innocence lost at the end of the former was never regained. Billy is blown away and left for dead at the side of the road, as his vehicle crashes and burns. A generation later, one of CeeBee's defining experiences is the traumatic crash that she has inexplicably survived.

Out Of The Blue could just as easily tell the story of what happened to Hopper's character in **Easy Rider** if he had not been shot, but instead reached middle age and lost the plot, got hitched, had a kid and swapped his bike for a Mack truck.

Hopper even made the link between the two films himself: "You could say the father and the mother probably saw **Easy Rider**, and that the father was probably a biker in his day."[4] In one early scene, CeeBee gives herself a home-made "Elvis" tattoo then burns a picture of Priscilla Presley and Elvis on their wedding day. As the flames consume the black and white image, they seem to lick at and split in half a framed picture behind it, of Kathy and Donny in happier times. Donny is wearing a '50s biker cap with a chain link across the rim, an iconic pose reminiscent of Marlon Brando in **The Wild One**.

The biker is to the punk what the beatnik was to the hippy. The latter dropped out of society while the former pushed beyond it. Having experienced all these four periods – through the '50s, '60s, '70s and '80s – Hopper is a canny manipulator of youth culture. Part of **Easy Rider**'s phenomenal success was the way it incorporated popular music as narrative commentary, almost single-handedly changing the nature of film soundtracks. In **Out Of The Blue**, Hopper again uses music as narrative commentary.

Surprisingly, there is very little in the way of actual punk rock on the soundtrack – apart from the ska-influenced punk played by the band CeeBee hangs out with on her sojourn to the city. There's the repetition of "Heartbreak Hotel" and "Teddy Bear", two melancholic tracks by Elvis that symbolise CeeBee's desire for a return to innocence and her fractured relationship to her parents. (Elvis is cited as "the original punk" in the narrative.) But the central musical motif is provided by Neil Young, whose soft-spoken social commentary and oft-times splintered squalls of guitar feedback was only re-evaluated as "punk" in the late '80s through the acknowledgment of his influence by "no-wave" noise punks Sonic Youth.

A long-time friend of Hopper's, Young offered to write an original song for the film, but in the end it was a track from his 1979 *Rust Never Sleeps* album that provided the film's main theme and title. Young's symbolic stripped-to-the-bone lyrics are so closely intertwined with the film's narrative that it's hard to believe Hopper wasn't riffing off the song as he made the movie; the words also help provide a self-reflective reading of the narrative.

Sung in Young's broken falsetto, **Out Of The Blue** is the haunting elegy to youthful nihilism that Kurt Cobain quoted in his suicide note – specifically the line, "It's better to burn out than to fade away". CeeBee echoes the same line in an act of wish fulfilment after she has been to see Donny in jail for the first time in five years. In her father's absence, she has idealised him as a rock and roll hero, sublimating her need for a father figure into an adolescent fixation of unattainable, male role models. She is obsessed

with the "comeback period", black leather-clad Elvis, who apes Donny's style, and Johnny Rotten, who represents his attitude and aggression. (In Young's song one couplet goes, "The King is gone but he's not forgotten. This is the story of Johnny Rotten".) But the man she sees in jail cannot live up to her ideal. Pitiful and weak, he has CeeBee ushered away by Kathy as the tears well up inside him.

The line in the song that refers to the title – "Out of the blue and into the black" – suggests numerous thematic possibilities within the narrative. "Blue" is associated with depression, sadness and gloom, indecency and pornography (in terms of film), manual labour (blue-collar), a clear sky, and denim (the staple of the rock and roller dress code). "Black" is also associated with gloom and depression, but also the night sky, darkness, the unknown and anything sinister. Black leather jackets are associated with rebel and outlaw characters.[5] Donny/Hopper represents the "blue". The trailer of his truck is painted a vibrant royal blue. He wears a blue waistcoat and passes a bottle of blue pills (possibly to treat depression ["blues"]) to CeeBee to keep her distracted in the truck. When Kathy and CeeBee visit him in jail, he is wearing a blue convict's workshirt. On release, he wears a denim jacket, jeans and a black t-shirt and works as a manual labourer, driving a bulldozer at the

city dump. The film is all about the ramifications of his "indecent assault" on his child and the ending is without doubt pornographic in its intensity. During her trip to the city, CeeBee is taken to the "Blue Motel" by the cab driver, who assumes the symbolic role of her father and tries to rape her as she sleeps.

CeeBee represents the "black". She has inherited Donny's dysfunction and more. Her future is muddied with his past. Most of the time, CeeBee wears faded blue denim jeans and jacket with a sequined guitar and Elvis' signature embroidered on the back, but when she wants to symbolically assume the role of the father – ideally as rock and roll icon, literally as truck driver and abuser – she puts Donny's biker cap, black leather jacket and boots on over her own clothes like a second skin.

On the most basic level, the transition from blue to black symbolises that of day to night and the onset of darkness (flash-forward to Hopper as Frank Booth in **Blue Velvet** – "now it's dark"). It also suggests a progressive discolouration of the flesh – in other words, a degradation of the body, which is also a description of one effect of Donny's sexual abuse – and an increase in the intensity of violence.

Hanging out in an ice cream parlour with two of her friends, CeeBee confronts Anderson's teenage daughter, after overhearing her badmouth Donny. She grabs the Anderson girl and smears her face with blue ice cream. "I painted your face blue," CeeBee says triumphantly. "And if you don't shut up and get outta here, I'm gonna take you out of the blue and put you into the black."

When CeeBee awakes in a cold sweat (from what we can safely assume is a repeating nightmare reliving the crash) there is a cut to the outside of the house. The sky is a bright break-of-dawn blue, speckled with wispy black clouds. The family home is seen entirely in silhouette, blacked-out apart from the light in CeeBee's window, immediately conjuring up its association as a dark place in which bad things are happening. Later in the narrative, when CeeBee is driving an over-crowded stolen car, we finally see the end of the crash sequence. As it ploughs into the yellow school bus, Donny's blue truck is shrouded in a black cloud of smoke.

Finally, the last verse of Young's song contains the lyric, "There's more to the picture than meets the eye". This gels with Hopper's description of the narrative as "like a little article on the fourth page of a newspaper that says a kid's killed her mother and father, and you wonder what that's about then move along."[6] The film's skewed production history has some significance to its final form. Originally Hopper was only hired to play the part of Donny. Leonard Yakir, one half of the script-writing team, was scheduled to direct it as a made-for-TV movie, for his directorial debut. But after two weeks of shooting, executive producer Paul Lewis (who had worked with Hopper on both **Easy Rider** and **The Last Movie**) saw nothing usable in the can and decided to walk. Having been thrown into Hollywood hinterland after the failure of **The Last Movie** – a crushing failure that some observers believe accelerated his personal problems – Hopper had not directed a film for almost ten years. Seeing an opportunity to direct, and thereby prove himself once again worthy to Hollywood, Hopper viewed the footage and offered to step into the director's shoes, on the proviso that he be allowed to revise the script to his own specifications and re-cast everyone but the principals.

At that time the film was called "The Case Of Cindy Barnes" and focused on a child psychologist's efforts to save a young girl from herself and her destructive family environment. The psychologist was played by Canadian actor Raymond Burr (of *Perry Mason* fame), who was appearing in the film to ensure its eligibility for one hundred percent tax relief under Canadian laws intended to promote its film industry and attract US productions across the border.

Hopper didn't like the script and specifically a voice-over narration by Burr's character that ran through it, making him the film's "hero". Instead he concentrated on the character of CeeBee, adding the crucial punk rock element and changed the ending, in which CeeBee originally killed only her father. "Why not kill them all?" Hopper thought, and so he did.

The drab industrial town setting (actually Vancouver) and naturalistic shooting style give the film a gritty realism unequalled in Hopper's other directorial efforts. A tight production schedule – the film was shot in four weeks and edited in two – meant improvising wherever possible. Hopper was particularly pleased with the one-shot sequences, something he had never tried before but included so that there was nothing to cut to if the producers tried to take the film back and dilute his vision, which finds its vile apotheosis in the film's ending. It is in the closing sequence that the narrative takes a sudden and cataclysmic downward spiral.

In an impressionistic montage of one-shots, Hopper drops the viewer right into heart of the family nightmare. CeeBee transforms herself into a grotesque identification with both parents – wearing her hair over-greased and slicked back, with drawn on side-burns, red lipstick and Don's biker duds. Confronted by a drunken, swaggering Donny, sneering "I'm a punk" as he terrorises them, mother and daughter are united in fear and loathing. In the terrifying final one-shot, CeeBee, dressed in her night-gown and smoking a joint, offers up her cotton panties for daddy to sniff. Head buried in her crotch, he moans and whimpers (prefiguring Frank Booth's baby-fixated fetishism in **Blue Velvet**). Holding Donny's head in place with one hand, CeeBee stabs him repeatedly with a pair of surgical scissors. The blood ejaculates out in arcs as Donny falls backwards. Cut dramatically to black.

In the final scene, CeeBee takes her mother out to the truck. She is again dressed in the biker uniform, but has now pierced her left cheek with a safety pin. She lights the fuse of the dynamite wedged into the dashboard. "This is senseless," Kathy screams hysterically. "That's right. That's right," CeeBee repeats blankly as the cab explodes in a fireball of familial angst.

Not surprisingly, Canada refused to let the film be entered into the Cannes Film Festival as a national entry. It appeared simply as "A Dennis Hopper film". Hopper was not welcomed back into Hollywood as he had hoped. He had succeeded in producing a calling card of such intense anger and self-loathing that any producer worth his salt would have run a mile rather than work with him. Hopper carried on making low-key indie movies, foreign features and TV movies until 1986, when his startling turn as Frank Booth in **Blue Velvet** codified the Dennis Hopper persona we know today and resurrected his mainstream career.

Although well received in Britain and Europe, **Out Of The Blue** had the effect of a particularly virulent emetic when it opened in America. "People were arguing and fighting, screaming and yelling at the screen," said

Hopper, describing what he saw at the Boston premiere[7], which sounds much like the furious exorcism that occurs at a punk gig. "[The film] seems to upset people in America – they take it really personally. When I got off the stage, I was surrounded by people and felt really scared: I felt I was John Lennon for a second." So, at least on some level, **Out Of The Blue** gratified Hopper's desire to become a rock and roll icon.

NOTES

1. "Dennis Hopper: A Madness To His Method" by Elena Rodriguez (St. Martin's Press, 1988) p130–1.

2. *Cinema Papers*, July 1987.

3. *Journal Of Popular Film And Television*, May 1983.

4. "Dennis Hopper: A Madness To His Method" by Elena Rodriguez (St. Martin's Press, 1988) p136.

5. The only other recurring colours, in an otherwise monochromatic movie, are yellow, orange and red, which are all suggestive of heat, fire and explosions. The cab of Donny's truck is yellow, as is the bulldozer he drives at the dump. Yellow walls and orange furnishings predominate in the family home. Donny's car is a red convertible. Hopper has famously asserted, on more than one occasion, that all his films end in fire, and the closing shot of the blue trailer burning in a shroud of black smoke incorporates all three colours.

6. "Dennis Hopper: A Madness To His Method" by Elena Rodriguez (St. Martin's Press, 1988) p136.

7. "Dennis Hopper: How Far To The Last Movie?", interview by Julian Petley and Peter Walsh (*Monthly Film Bulletin*, Oct. 1982) p222.

"HOPPERALITY": DENNIS HOPPER AND 'TEXAS CHAINSAW MASSACRE 2'

"...it's great to look over your shoulder and see the young you there... it's like a dream."[1]

In the new television advertisement for the Ford Cougar a greying, sharply dressed [sic] Dennis Hopper has an encounter with a spirit from his rebellious youth in the shape of his hippy biker character, "Billy", from **Easy Rider**. Or should that read: on the road in **Easy Rider**, a young Dennis Hopper has an encounter with a spirit from his older, calmer, more conservative future driving a Ford Cougar. It is a curious encounter to say the least, a brief, bright flickering of CGI shadows that adumbrates a set of historical and, for Hopper himself, personal contradictions. Of course the picture is further complicated by the fact that Hopper Sr. occupies the space formerly taken up with Peter Fonda (and his chopper) who has, like Leon Trotsky from old Politburo photographs, been elided from the image. When the young Hopper looks over to smile at Fonda, it is now the new/old Hopper who grins back. He then accelerates away, leaving his other self, his radical past and "absent friends" as nothing more than hazy reflections, shrinking fast in the car's bright mirror.[2]

Apparently, the original concept for the Cougar campaign was to have reunited both Hopper and Fonda in their **Easy Rider** personae, as Leighton Ballett and Lee Goulding from agency Young and Rubicam explain: "Our initial proposition for the new coupe was the idea of 'Wild at Heart', which led us to **Easy Rider** and Dennis Hopper... The original idea was for two Ford Cougars driven across the desert by Peter Fonda and Dennis Hopper, seen re-living their past, and set to the original music from **Easy Rider**, 'Born To Be Wild'. Using special FX we hoped they would meet up with their younger selves, thus showing off the car and capturing the spirit of being 'Wild at Heart'. All summed up with the thought, 'Ford Cougar, Easy Driver'."[3]

Apart from missing the point of the film completely, the men from the agency clearly (if perhaps unsurprisingly) have only the shakiest grasp of film history, reacting with surprise when they discovered that complex human relationships would get in the way of CGI "simplicity": "Unfortunately when we approached Fonda's agent we were told he'd vowed never to work with Hopper again – they had a big bust up over the original movie apparently!"[4] This was not, of course, a problem encountered with the previous campaign for the Ford Puma, resurrecting as it did as a distinctly uncanny digital revenant, a young Steve McQueen for a s(l)ick pastiche of **Bullitt**.

McQueen, of course, died young and, as Hopper himself freely admits, by rights he should have died also. However, decades of calculated (and not-so-calculated) alcoholic and narcotic excess built onto an addictive personality finally led to two attempts at drying out – notably in 1984 at Cedars Sinai Medical Centre's substance abuse programme – and, against all the odds, Hopper survived. His re-emergence "clean and sober" initiated a period of feverish professional activity in the mid to late 1980s which included critically acclaimed performances such as his Frank Booth in **Blue Velvet** and the part of an ex-alcoholic basketball coach in **Best Shot** (aka **Hoosiers**), for which he was nominated for an Oscar. In a typically wry reflection on his work in the latter film, Hopper has commented: "I'm not sure if it was acting... or total recall".[5] And again of this and similar performances: "It was a role I've rehearsed for years."[6]

During the mid-1980s, Hopper also acted in a number of films for which he did not receive much in the way of mainstream critical attention. Perhaps the most consistently – not to say pointedly – ignored of his acting efforts in this period (ignored not least by Hopper himself) was the part of Texas Ranger "Lefty" Enright in Tobe Hooper's **Texas Chainsaw Massacre 2**. Hopper's attitude to his own performance in this film and the fan responses it provoked can, however, serve as an interesting model for understanding the trajectory of his later career – the trajectory that finally led him to the Ford Cougar ad.

In the mid-1980s, however, his phenomenal work-rate can be put down to a number of complementary issues which can perhaps be dovetailed into the coincidence of his becoming employable in industry terms once again (for reasons of both health and "attitude") and, from a personal viewpoint, an overwhelming desire to make up for lost time. Barbra Paskin quotes him to this effect in a piece written in 1988: "I feel like a baby. I feel really good. There's a lot of work and I'm happy about that when I have time to think about it. Usually I'm too busy working. But whenever I feel I'm working too much, I remember all those years when I just sat there and wondered if I'd ever work again. I've got a lot of catching up to do."[7]

Hopper's personal and professional "rebirth" found him developing a new approach to his own practice and in particular to his job as an actor. In his youth he was notoriously "difficult". The story of his conflict with Henry Hathaway on the set of **From Hell To Texas** which, in part, led to him being blacklisted in Hollywood has become a central pillar of the Hopper legend. Hopper's version, according to his biographer, accuses Hathaway of asking him to copy Brando: "And I'd say 'I don't want to do that, I'm trying to get away from that, and please don't give me line readings. I'm a method actor.

I work with my ears, my sight, my head, and my sense of smell'."[8]

Hopper has always been very precious about his status as an actor, and particularly concerning his passionate allegiance to "the Method": a theory of, and training in the acting process developed from the work of the Russian stage actor and director Constantin Stanislavski (1863–1938) by Lee Strasberg and others at The Actors Studio in New York. It is abundantly clear from his interviews and other sources that the young Hopper was deeply, even fundamentally transformed as a creative artist by his first encounters with the Method and with those of his contemporaries who were, in their turn, inspired by its promise of apparent truth and reality in acting:

"Observing Dean and Clift I realised I'd have to be a rebel and a fighter. It seemed to me that's what you had to be if you wanted to be a good artist. You had to fight directors when they told you how to play something. Dean taught me how to act from my senses. Directors are like schoolmarms, everything is set in their minds, they give you every gesture to do, and to find your own space in your own way you have to say 'Wait a moment, I don't work that way; I don't put the cigarette in this hand, or walk like this. I do moment-to-moment things.' But they said 'Not on my film you don't'."[9]

He credits James Dean in particular for introducing him to that training: "I literally picked him up, threw him into the car, and said, 'What are you doing? How can I do it? Do I have to go to Strasberg? Do I have to go to New York? Look man, I gotta know how you act 'cause you're the greatest.' Jimmy said, 'No, no take it easy man. Just listen to me and I'll help you along. Do things, don't show them. Stop the gestures. In the beginning everything will be very difficult because you're used to acting. But pretty soon it will be natural to you and you'll start going and the emotions will come to you if you leave yourself open to the moment-to-moment reality'."[10]

The influence of Stanislavski on American theatre and film acting has been both long term and contested. Indeed his ideas have been interpreted in a number of ways, although arguably the most influential, not to say controversial threads have connected the work of the American Lab Theater (1920s) to that of the Group Theater (1930s) and thence to the consolidation of what might hesitantly be called a post-Stanislavski training into the "orthodoxy" of Strasberg's interpretation at The Actors Studio (founded in 1947). Not all Actors Studio members were of a mind regarding Strasberg's approach. At least two of the founding members of the Studio, Robert Lewis and Elia Kazan, were opposed both to Strasberg and to his ideas – indeed after Lewis left in 1948, Kazan did his best to prevent Strasberg from teaching at the Studio.

The Method isn't Stanislavski. Or rather it is Stanislavski recalibrated by the industry of American popular Freudianism. So while for Stanislavski the core experience of acting involves the performer in an imaginative connection with the circumstances of the play, the Method focuses on emotional responses derived from the actor's personal experiences which are accessed through techniques such as "affective memory" exercises: "Stanislavski stressed imagination as the core of acting, and sought emotional truth from the text of the play. Strasberg sought emotional truth from the unconscious of the actor. This approach, which was highly controversial, had particular appeal and power in cinema, where close-up acting underscored the intimacy of a scene. Stanislavski's original emphasis on inner technique and intellectual technique (script analysis) was incorporated into the Method but the physicality of the system was totally dismissed, and replaced by analytical considerations. According to Strasberg, the actor must be free of inhibitions to achieve emotional truthfulness. The same emotional truthfulness was achieved by Stanislavski through the justified and motivated 'logic of physical actions' which was never explored by Strasberg."[11]

The debate over the use or reliance upon affective memory work is the issue which divided Strasberg from many of the principal American exponents of the Stanislavskian approach. Stella Adler, for example, largely dismissed such work other than specifically in relation to the text at hand, while Sanford Meisner "...shared the original stress on imagination as the key to spontaneity. Instead of probing the unconscious, he advocated an imaginative 'fantasy' which could be developed and controlled by the actor."[12] Harold Clurman has, perhaps, put the contra position outlining the value and also the typical misuse of affective memory work most eloquently: "...in the cultivation and use of affective memory (interrelated with memory of the senses) Stanislavsky [sic] found the authentic stuff of life with which acting must be informed... In the memory of emotions Stanislavsky discovered the usable 'roots' within the actor's person which might be guided toward the making of that new personality which is a particular role of a play. The purpose and goal of this technique was to fulfil the *play* – not just the actor. Those who suppose that Stanislavsky was not concerned with the dramatist's work simply don't know what they are talking about or they have mistaken Stanislavsky's apes for the man himself... In the United States the stress on emotional memory was embraced as a saving grace, as a universal answer. It became a fetish. It was what we all sought, were in need of *feeling*. That is why the Method for many American actors is no longer a technique but a therapy."[13]

Stanislavski's system parallels the *work on the self* and the *work on the part*. If the Method over privileges the former – if the Method is therapy – then Hopper is perhaps its most obvious and public patient. His own position on the training is typically idiosyncratic, however. In his accounts of his own approach to acting, Hopper characterises the key teachings of Adler,

Meisner and Strasberg with undeniable passion, but also with a certain ambiguity:

"You're basically breaking it down into three things. You have your subconscious, you have your imagination, and you have your senses. And so Stella [Adler] who was Marlon's teacher, came back and said everything you can find through the object. If you work with the object, it will make your imagination happen and your senses will be affected and you will reach your subconscious. So use objects. You'll notice when Brando acts, he is always working with objects of one kind or another. So this is one way you can break down and reach your subconscious."

"[Sanford] Meisner," Dennis continued, "said it's your imagination. You get your imagination working properly, it will stimulate your senses and by stimulating your senses you will reach your subconscious like little kids playing in a field: 'Bang, bang, you're dead.' 'No you missed me.' 'Yeah I got you.' [Lee] Strasberg said it's the senses. If you develop your senses through sense memory and then go into emotional memory, then your imagination will work and you will reach you subconscious... Because the hardest thing in the world is first to be in front of an audience, but then to reach your subconscious through a conscious means is almost impossible. I mean, you can say, Oh my God. My mother, when she died, or when my father died – But it has no meaning to your subconscious. Thinking about the very fact that you felt at the time that this actually happened. So you have to trick yourself through asking, 'What was I wearing?' or not 'What was I wearing?' but 'Can I feel what I was wearing that day, was it hot that day, can I feel some of that heat? The sound, what was I hearing?' And through that, rather than relating to the incident, you can then trick your subconscious into reacting, through whatever given sense. And then you can do your scene."[14]

Although it is perhaps unfair to second guess Hopper's position on the basis of his somewhat cryptic statements in interviews, it does appear that his notion of objects implicitly combines the ideas of character goal and physical article. In other words, he gives the impression of conflating dramatic intention; played emotion and its physical manifestation or externalisation into a single, complex (not to say conflicted) psychological 'knot'. Indeed, his statements about acting are shot through with a powerful series of assertions about the primacy of sensory input. Once again: "I work with my ears, my sight, my head, and my sense of smell." Even in discussing his past addictions he frequently brings the subject back around to the senses: "I guess I did it because all the people I admired were drug addicts and alcoholics. I felt if they were doing it then it must lead to something. It does help you with your senses; it makes them like raw nerves. And when you're working with your senses you want them right at your fingertips so that you can use them."[15]

This sense of immediacy, this fundamentally sensual, even libidinal mind-set manifests itself in Hopper's physicality as an actor. Frank Booth's restless hands fondle the scrap of blue velvet torn from Dorothy's dress. Nervous hands express the impossibility of putting Kurtz' megalomaniacal excesses into sane language in **Apocalypse Now**. Again and again that disturbing, contorting nasal paroxysm – the snorting ingestion of real world stimulus for transformation into "mad matter" that punctuates the speech and actions of a long list of Hopper's psychopaths and losers. Hopper's characters fix on life as they wallow in death and depravity and it is this paradox above all that often makes a Hopper performance so magnetic. Edward Murphy, writing in *Film Review*, articulates this exact connection in rather starstruck terms: "Very few actors today have the ability to burn a hole with screen presence, but Dennis Hopper is that unique talent whose personal lifestyle, at one point, seemed to manifest itself as raging torrents throughout his performances."[16] Of course one consequence of this perception of Hopper as the half-tamed maniac of Method acting is that he has been cast in a limited range of roles. This is clearly an issue that concerns him, although he takes pains to distance himself from the implication that he simply plays to type: "People say I play the same characters – weird and deranged – and I think it's generally true... I play them differently but I play deranged people. You have a greater emotional range with them. But then, again, they're the only kind of roles I'm offered."[17]

His "Lefty" Enright certainly falls into the above category. The scenario for **Texas Chainsaw Massacre 2** involves Hopper's character's obsessive hunt for the killers of his wheelchair-bound nephew, a victim from the original film. Although his screen time is limited – Hopper gets top billing, but the leading role goes to Caroline Williams' Radio DJ, "Stretch" Brock – Hopper's energised performance is consistently mobilised as a central attraction. The film revels in excess all the way through, from its underlying theme of cannibal catering, via its explicit satire on violence in American culture to the intensity of its revenge plot. Physical excess is built in through Tom Savini's gory makeup effects and the film's narrative frequently pauses for displays of violence, but also for Hopper's acting set pieces.

The scene in which Enright goes to buy chainsaws and tests them out is a particular case in point. Along with the owner of the store, we watch unnerved as Hopper mimes a chainsaw duel and then sets about a tree trunk with manic abandon. Indeed, the store owner seems quite bewildered and uneasy from the moment Enright enters the store – but then the actor had presumably just seen Hopper's rehearsal... The scene holds and holds as Enright continues feverishly to saw into the wood and we are left with the distinct impression that, in the film's terms at least, this moment is presented to the audience as an equivalent instance of excessive pleasure to the killings and other moments of terror and horror that regularly punctuate the narrative. Of course Hopper's contorted face and whirling saw also sets up a direct parallel to Leatherface's repeated frenzied whirling. We are meant to infer that the Sawyers are about to meet their match, in madness if not in handed down slaughterhouse technique. When you have Hopper's crazy face, the film is telling us, who needs to wear someone else's. Acting and star presence have always been staple attractions of the cinema, but in this film the idea of star-as-attraction is being taken a step further. It is not so much the quality of Hopper's characterisation of Enright, nor for that matter a general, associated aura of personality or appearance (in the Cary Grant sense) that is on display, as it is the direct equation of Hopper-as-Hopper with Hopper-as-madness.

Recent fan criticism of his role in **Texas Chainsaw Massacre 2** does nothing to dissuade one from this assertion. A broad, if somewhat unscientific trawl through horror fan websites yields an interesting pattern of comments. Opinion regarding the quality of the film itself is split sharply between those who approve of the comedic turn that the sequel has taken and (the majority of the sites I hit) and those who view it as an unforgivable betrayal of the aesthetic of the original **The Texas Chain Saw Massacre**. This divergence of opinion notwithstanding, however, most fans single out Hopper's performance for praise. Their comments serve to highlight the ascendency of what, *pace* Philip Brophy, we might (with tongue in cheek) call "Hopperality" over Hopper himself. By Hopperality I mean the reduction of Hopper to the trope of madness and the deployment of that trope (by the casting of Hopper-as-special-effect) across a range of films: "This movie does have a couple of frightening parts, but is mostly just an entertaining flick with some great acting by Dennis Hopper. Some may consider his performance a little over-the-top, but when is he not? That's his *trademark*."[18] [My italics] "...Dennis Hopper [not, we note, "Lefty: Enright...] tracks them to their lair and proves that he is just as crazy as they are."[19] "At least Dennis Hopper saves the film some face – hamming it up like a giant leg of pork."[20]

American press reviews paint a somewhat different picture. Typically, either the film is praised for the satirical intent of L. M. Kit Carson's script or dismissed pretty much out of hand as exploitative and excessive. Hopper's performance, indeed the acting in general, is often used to back up this latter position. Leonard Maltin's review is scathing, for example, although the material is hardly designed to appeal to his sensibilities: "Frenetic overacting and unfunny attempts at black humour sink this mess."[21] Roger Ebert who, given his own background and his avowed affection for **The Texas Chain Saw Massacre**, one would expect to have at least some sympathy for Tobe Hooper's project, is also less than impressed. He too is dismissive of Hopper's performance, although he fixes the blame in part on poor writing: "Dennis Hopper has the most thankless task, playing a man who spends the first half

of the movie looking distracted and vague, and the second half screaming during chainsaw duels."[22] *Variety*, on the other hand gave the film a very positive critique, its reviewer clearly enjoying Hopper's performance: "Packing chainsaw sixguns in a holster at his side, Hopper has the zeal of a fundamentalist preacher setting out to clean up the filth."[23]

The genre press, at least in the shape of Alan Jones writing in *Starburst* were more sympathetic. Jones is enthusiastic about the film and his is one of the only reviews I have come across which has no comment to make about Hopper's acting other than to refer to the character as "...an obsessive evangelical ex-Texas Ranger...", a comment which implies Hopperality without actually invoking it.[24] Not all of his fans are enthusiastic about the re-born Hopper, however. William Tyler Smith, a filmmaker and long-time Hopper fan from New York dismisses his recent career in the following terms. "He's become a joke. He's become the 'Toys R Us' Action Doll of Method acting..."[25]

To criticise, marginalise and/or dismiss Hopper merely for excess like mainstream critics have tended to do is, finally, a reductive response. There is, indeed, a convincing argument to be made for the place of excess in film acting. While acknowledging historically bound non-naturalistic approaches such as can be found in Expressionism or Surrealism, we can easily follow for a distance Carole Zucker's formulation that excess in the diegesis allows excess in characterisation. Zucker is looking in particular at Crispin Glover's idiosyncratic performance in **Twister** (1990) and Nicholas Cage's faux-Expressionist acting style in **Vampire's Kiss** (1988): "All acting is, in a sense the word incarnated in flesh, and our absorption in the performance largely depends on the actor's abilities, and further, on his or her capacity to choose creatively and well. The criteria by which these choices are more or less apt hinges on the style and demands of the narrative, i.e., in a narrative that is closer on the spectrum to realism, the criteria of 'truthfulness' and 'naturalness', would obtain. But in cases such as the ones we are investigating, the diegetic world presents a very heightened or otherwise distorted version of reality. Thus, the style of acting – governed by this weakened resemblance to the world we know – is not bound by the laws of naturalistic behaviour. And where the stricture to play naturalistically is relaxed, the style of performance may be inclined, in more interesting cases, to 'excess', to a de-familiarized notion of human behaviour. This behaviour, moreover, may begin to take on a life of its own, well beyond the demands of the narrative structure."[26]

In other words: the less mimetic the work at hand, the greater the freedom for the actor in performance. As far as our present example goes then so far so good.; **Texas Chainsaw Massacre 2** is hardly naturalistic. But in Cage's choices in **Vampire's Kiss** at least, a very specific, historical body of work is being interrogated, notably the performance of Max Schreck in F.W. Murnau's **Nosferatu** (1922). Hopper, it could be argued, is simply playing Hopper in his best work and playing *at* Hopper in his less accomplished performances. This is not much of an issue for a classical Hollywood star like Bogart, Grant or Wayne, nor perhaps for many Hopper fans, but for a method actor achieving a general "quality' of self is not enough. Hopper has very little to say about his own work on **Texas Chainsaw Massacre 2**, and what he does say is dismissive. Elena Rodriguez' brief reference to the film starts like this: "Dennis went on to do another 'scary' movie that he did not have to take seriously, but it was employment that kept the cash coming in... He later gave his own critique of the film, saying: 'I was lousy – it's a lousy film, but I had fun doing it'."[27] The point of all this, once again, is to document the shift in Hopper's position in relation to his work – indeed that is just the point, in the mid-1980s mere work regularly began to be allowed, for all the usual prosaic reasons: "I'm not difficult now, I'm not out to steal any scenes, I don't cause people to go over budget... I have technique enough to adapt my style, to work in a given format. If you try and do things differently, you stand out as a sore thumb or a pain, and I'd rather not be either one. I realise the director's the director; what he says, the actor better do. You don't come to direct, that's not your business... It took me a while to learn that."[28]

The Hopperality argument, based on **Texas Chainsaw Massacre 2** and other similar performances (**River's Edge** included), would suggest that Hopper's "return from the dead" clean-and-sober is marked by the not so gradual conventionalisation and commodification of his image. It is a process which leads straight to the Ford Cougar advertisement of 1998/9 and, thus, to this moment of writing. Dennis Hopper's fans and supporters have at various points in his career gone to great lengths to justify his style. Barbara Scharres, writing in 1983 just at the cusp of the period of Hopper's revival, offers an account of his acting and directing which makes virtues of what others have claimed as vices: "Hopper does not have a wide range, either as an actor or director. If the complete scope of human emotions were represented on a linear scale, only the two extremes would reflect the concentration of his portrayals and directorial concerns. Hopper's work is about extremes, it is about broad gestures and characters who cannot comprehend culturally imposed and emotional restraints. There is no middle range, where 'realistic' portrayals can be found in his work, and he is one of the few American directors to continually explore emotional violence."[29]

Of course Hopper's re-emergence as a director has subsequently given the lie to the notion that he lacks range in this area. Whatever critical judgement can be applied to each and all of them, to have directed films as diverse as **The Last Movie**, **Out Of The Blue**, **Colors** and even **Chasers** certainly necessitates a high level of professional flexibility. As to his acting career, perhaps Joanne Woodward had something when she said of him: "Dennis is a genius. I'm not sure of what, and I'm not sure Dennis knows of what. Certainly not acting. But he is a genius."[30] My personal connection to that statement came when I was searching for Dennis Hopper sites on the Internet recently. I came upon a website with the tag: "Insane Actor Stalks **Speed** Star". My first and immediate reaction was: "Oh dear, what has Dennis been up to now..." only to find that of course it was Hopper who was the one being stalked! For me to have so deeply internalised the equation of Hopper and madness probably finally says more about me than it does about his possible genius but, as we have seen, for a great many people that equation stands. What I have been attempting to work through is, perhaps a change in the product of the equation: a change from possible savant to licensed fool.

And yet I would submit that there has been a curious, even endearing consistency in Hopper's personal and career choices – good and bad, creative and pragmatic. From his desperation to learn from James Dean, through his desire to follow his peers into drugs and alcohol to find out where it was leading them, to his recently avowed and newly minted professionalism, Hopper's life can be seen actually, and perversely, to have been characterised in part by a very strong impulse to "fit in". He has perhaps picked an odd and eclectic range of groups and contexts in which to fit, but his apparently meandering path through left-field has a certain inevitable logic to it. The journey from **Easy Rider** to Ford Cougar was not, perhaps, as long as at first it seems. When Hopper watches himself looking over at his younger self in the Ford Cougar advertisement he may reflect that the intervening years only actually required that the young Dennis Hopper fail to "bite the **Bullitt**" for this meeting, or one very much like it, to be a logical squaring of the circle. The absence from the picture of erstwhile partner, Peter Fonda, however, may perhaps cause him to reflect in his own way on the politics of his choices.[31]

NOTES

1. "Easy Rider Drives Again... Dennis Hopper Stars In Sequel Ad With... Dennis Hopper" (publicity for the Ford Cougar campaign) at: www.rushes.co.uk/post/Latest/FordCougar.html.

2. Echoes of Hopper's role in **Flashback** (Franco Amurri, 1990), in which he plays an ageing '60s radical on the run, who changes identity with his conservative, smart-suited FBI pursuer to avoid capture.

3. Ibid.

4. Ibid.

5. Press kit for **Colors**, Rank Film Distributors 1988, p.9.

6. Ibid. p.16.

7. Barbra Paskin "Den Of Iniquity", *Options For Men* October 1988, p.16.

8. Elena Rodriguez *A Madness To His Method*, New York: St. Martin's Press, 1988, p.36.

9. Paskin, 1988, p.14.

10. Rodriguez, 1988, p.20.

11. Richard A. Blum *American Film Acting: The Stanislavski Heritage*, Ann Arbor: UMI Research Press, 1984, p.52.

12. Ibid. p.54.

13. Harold Clurman *On Directing*, Macmillan: New York, 1972, p.151. Clurman is particularly scathing about what have come down to us as the clichés of Method performance: "When an actor mumbles, behaves in all sorts of unseemly and distasteful ways, grovels shamelessly, forces his soul grotesquely, cries out and roars to the point of unintelligibility, it is not because he is a 'Method actor' but because he is a bad actor. No English or French theatre schooling has ever been as exacting in its insistence on vocal flexibility, control, euphony, clarity, force and beauty of speech as Stanislavsky." (p.149.)

14. A BBC interview with Hopper cited in Rodriguez, p.162.

15. Paskin, 1988, p.14–16.

16. Edward Murphy "Hopping Mad", *Film Review* November 1988.

17. Paskin, 1988, p.16. As an aside, Lee Strasberg's particular interpretation of Stanislavski's work also moved away from the Russian's resistance to the issue of typecasting. Strasberg maintained that "...it maximized awareness of the character and eased the merger process of self with character." (Blum, 1984, p.52.) Blum makes the point that typecasting is to a certain

extent, of course, made pretty much inevitable in film by the special requirements of actorly credibility and realism and, thus, the question of Hopper's being pigeonholed into playing detectives and maniacs – from which, as we shall see, he draws significant personal and professional conclusions – can be seen to have at least a partially intellectual basis. Incidentally I do not wish to give the impression that Strasberg is entirely alone in this regard. On the contrary, Harold Clurman amongst others also acknowledges the value of typing in the theatre: "...though actors resent the emphasis on 'type', there are parts in which the right physical image (along with ability) is very nearly decisive." (Clurman, 1972, p.69.) Clurman goes on to cite the casting of Yelena in *Uncle Vanya* as a particular, if perhaps superficial, example of this. "The credibility of *Uncle Vanya*, for example, is considerably weakened if the audience does not share in both Astrov's and Voinitsky's intense appreciation of Yelena's magnetic attractiveness."

18. The quote is from a fan review found at: http://www.angrybear.com/tcmnet/tcm2rl.html. The reference to Brophy acknowledges his use of the term "horrality" to imply the increasing tendency in cinema to deploy horror tropes across other genres in a broadly modal (and potentially post-generic) context. (Philip Brophy *Horrality: The Textuality Of Contemporary Horror Films*, Screen Vol.27 #1, Jan–Feb 1986.)

19. The quote is from a fan review found at: http://members.aol.com/coffin13/chainsaw.html.

20. The quote is from a fan review by Jared Terry (bsassjte@cornwall.ac.uk) cited in the Internet Movie Database at: http://us.imdb.com/Title?Texas+Chainsaw+Massacre+2+The+ (110/2/1999).

21. Leonard Maltin's review at: http://us.imdb.com/Title?Texas+Chainsaw+Massacre+2+The+ (110/2/1999).

22. Roger Ebert's review at: http://us.imdb.com/Title?Texas+Chainsaw+ Massacre+2+The+ (110/2/1999).

23. *Variety*, August 27, 1986.

24. Alan Jones "Preview", *Starburst* #99.

25. Personal correspondence with the author, 1999.

26. Carole Zucker "The Concept of 'Excess' In Film Acting: Notes Towards An Understanding of Non-Naturalistic Performance", *Post Script* Vol.12 #2 p.56.

27. Rodriguez, 1988, p.172.

28. From an article by Kenneth Turan: "Dennis Hopper, A Survivor Of The '60s, Tries Again" (source unknown).

29. Barbara Scharres "From Out Of The Blue: The Return Of Dennis Hopper", *Journal Of The University Film And Video Association* Vol.35 #2, Spring 1983, p.27. Scharres goes on: "Hopper has an amazing talent for taking the most obvious symbols, trappings and behaviour of a

chosen time and situation and infusing them with brash originality as if they were the only examples of their kind. Because he often works with elements which in other usage were clichés, it is sometimes mistakenly assumed that he deals in clichés himself" (p.27.)

30. From an interview by Guy Lessor in the *Sunday Times Magazine* April 25, 1993.

31. As another fan, Tony Moon from Brighton puts it: "If Altamont was the spiritual death of the '60s, then the Ford Cougar commercial is the corpse being kicked around" (personal correspondence with the author, 1999). As a final example of his personal and professional transformation I offer these anecdotes. Dennis Hopper's 50th birthday fell during the shoot for **Texas Chainsaw Massacre 2**. As a celebration, the crew gave him a cake and a chainsaw to cut it with! Not unreasonably, he spent his birthday off-set, playing in a charity golf tournament with Willie Nelson. It was his second year clean of drugs. During the Ford Cougar shoot, when the production fell behind schedule because of bad weather, Hopper gave up his birthday to shoot an extra day.

"A CANDY-COLORED CLOWN...": DENNIS HOPPER IN 'BLUE VELVET'

David Lynch's **Blue Velvet** (1986) is set in Lumberton, which, on the surface, is the archetypal American small town; a community signified by white-picket fences, blue skies, and family values, the realization of a Norman Rockwell painting[1]. **Blue Velvet** focuses on all-American college boy Jeffrey Beaumont (Kyle MacLachlan) who is in Lumberton to run the family hardware store following his father's hospitalization. While returning from a visit to the hospital, Jeffrey finds a severed human ear which he takes to the police. Detective Williams (George Dickerson) warns Jeffrey not to tell anybody about the grisly find, but Jeffrey – his curiosity piqued – begins to investigate the ear, assisted by Detective Williams' teenage daughter Sandy (Laura Dern).

As the investigation continues Jeffrey finds that the ear has been severed from Don Vallens as a warning to his wife, nightclub chanteuse Dorothy (Isabella Rossellini), who is the sexual slave to criminal sadist Frank Booth (Dennis Hopper). Jeffrey rapidly finds himself dragged into the psycho-sexual undertow of the Booth/Vallens relationship, and into the increasingly dangerous Lumberton criminal underworld. His obsession with Vallens and Booth reaches a climax when he becomes Booth's unwilling passenger during a forced tour of the sleazy side of town, during which Jeffrey meets the ambiguously gendered gangster Ben (Dean Stockwell) with whom Booth works. This night-time drive culminates in Jeffrey receiving a vicious beating.

Vowing to quit his investigations and pursue his relationship with Sandy, Jeffrey is dragged back into a final showdown with Frank Booth following his discovery of a bruised and naked Dorothy wandering the night-time streets of Lumberton. David Lynch summarizes the film as about "a guy who lives in two worlds at the same time, one which is pleasant and the other dark and terrifying"[2].

Much has been written about **Blue Velvet** in psychoanalytic terms[3], suggesting that the film is constructed primarily as an Oedipal thriller which explores the three fundamental psychoanalytical phantasies: the primal scene, seduction, and castration. It is these phantasies which, in psychoanalytical terms, form the mise-en-scène to the Oedipus phase of infantile sexual development[4]. These phantasies deal with the central enigmas of childhood, and each deals with the question of origins; the primal scene represents the origin of the subject, seduction represents the emergence of sexuality, and castration marks the origin of sexual difference[5]. Jeffrey is thus on a quest into the darkness of the human psyche in order to resolve these fundamental

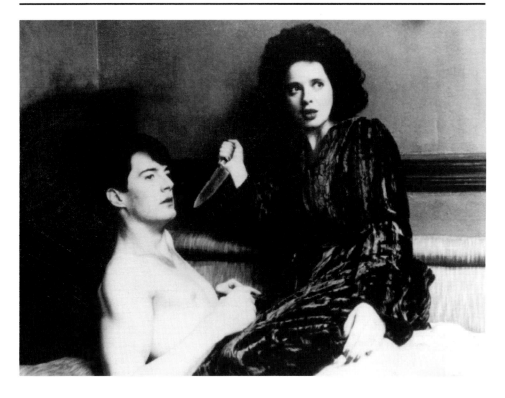

questions, as he states to Sandy "I'm seeing something that was always hidden"[6].

In **Blue Velvet** these phantasies are enacted through the triadic Jeffrey/Frank/Dorothy relationship – with Jeffrey acting as the child to the (dysfunctional) parents Frank and Dorothy. Jeffrey develops a relationship with Dorothy – recalling the phantasy of seduction, during which the child imagines himself to be seduced by his mother. Jeffrey spies sexual intercourse between the couple, whilst he hides, crouching in the closet, recalling the primal scene in which the child watches his parents copulate.

From his vantage point Jeffrey sees Frank violently fuck Dorothy, throwing her to the floor, snapping scissors over her body and face, punching her, cutting a segment from her gown, and stuffing both his own and Dorothy's mouth with a strip of blue velvet (Freud suggested the child at first may have a "sadistic misunderstanding of coition. ...if he finds traces of blood on his mother's bed or underclothes, he takes it as a sign that she has been injured by his father"[7]). Notably, during this sequence, Frank demands that he be referred to as "Daddy" and "Baby" – and speaks in both childlike and adult voices – and he refers to Dorothy as "Mummy".

Finally there is the phantasy of castration, this is the central element to the Oedipal phase, and the development of childhood sexuality. **Blue**

Velvet is rich in multiple images of castration; throughout the sexual molestation of Dorothy by Frank he wields scissors over her body, at one point snapping them over her crotch. The severed ear also signifies a form of castration – the loss of a part of the body – and Jeffrey's father, hooked up to machines in the hospital yet unable to move, also signifies a form of emasculation. More apparent themes of castration include the threat Raymond (Brad Dourif) a member of Frank's entourage, gives Jeffrey: "Here today—" (he snaps open a short bladed flick-knife) "gone tomorrow".

Yet the vertiginous psychosis of **Blue Velvet** also steps beyond the cold, fixed, triadic confines of the Oedipal scenario, into a world of transgression, dreams, nightmare, doubles, and pure atavism.

"IN DREAMS I WALK WITH YOU"

In the essay "Das Unheimliche" (*The Uncanny*, 1919) Sigmund Freud traces the relationship between the duality of the *heimlich* (homely) and *unheimlich*, a relationship in which far from being the polar opposites – despite the etymological suggestion – the two concepts melt and combine, with no fixed point of division between them. As Freud himself is forced to recognize, the *heimlich* "develops in the direction of ambivalence, until it finally coincides with its opposite"[8]. The uncanny is, in part, the familiar becoming unfamiliar, becoming pregnant with a different, transformed meaning. Throughout Freud's essay the certainty of that which is understood as uncanny becomes murky as it shades into the familiar, as "something which ought to have remained hidden but has come to light"[9]. The uncanny – at points – is recognized by Freud as the return of those aspects of the conscious that have been repressed: animism, the double, and the infantile fears, including – of course – castration.

Blue Velvet plays on this shading of the familiar to the unfamiliar – and the twilight relationship between light and dark. Lumberton is a town in which – just below the ever-so-ordinary surface – both physical and psychological – there exists a seething dark mass of unrestrained behaviour – from the scurrying fighting ants below the Beaumont's dream-clean yard in the film's opening scene, to the twisted psyches of the town's villains. Familiar landscapes shift and transform – from white wooden houses to shady apartment blocks, from teenagers in Arleen's Diner to sleazy back rooms filled with greasy-looking women – Lumberton is a town in which the social and the geographical slide. It is a community which transforms at dusk from small-town USA – the storehouse of American values – to a dangerous zone more recognizable to the audience as a portrayal of criminal degeneracy on 42nd Street or Times Square in seventies New York City.

Freud's study of the uncanny includes a detailed analysis of E.T.A

Hoffman's tale *The Sandman*. This is a story which focuses on a figure who rips out the eyes from children who won't go to bed, and feeds them to his own children. For Freud the tale is uncanny because it recalls the castration anxiety via the metaphor of the removal of the eyes. The narrative's central character is a boy – Nathaniel – who is determined to see the mythological figure of the Sandman, and thus hides "in an open cupboard just beside... where my father's clothes were hung... taking my courage in both hands, I peered cautiously out..."[10]. The parallel between the first appearance of the Sandman in Hoffman's text, and the initial presentation of Frank Booth in **Blue Velvet**, is clear.

Frank is further identified with the uncanny figure of the Sandman during a sequence in which Jeffrey is kidnapped and forced to spend an evening with Booth and his colleagues as they go and visit Ben in whose apartment Dorothy's son, Little Donny, is being held hostage. The evening ends – for Jeffrey – on a quiet road on the outskirts of town, where he is beaten by Booth. Prior to being punched Jeffrey is pinned to the side of a car by Booth. Booth has lipstick smeared across his mouth, and kisses Jeffrey, caressing his face with a ripped square of blue velvet, once again emasculating Jeffrey, who is rendered as castrated/object by Booth's actions. A hooker dances on the car's roof and the stereo blares Roy Orbison's song "In Dreams". Booth accompanies the song by stating each line of the chorus

as a statement-of-fact-threat to Jeffrey: "In dreams I walk with you/in dreams you are mine all the time". The first line of the song: "A candy coloured clown they call the Sandman".

Like the Sandman of Hoffman's tale, Booth is associated with something forbidden. As Nathaniel stayed up too late in order to catch a glimpse of the Sandman, the figure responsible for the removal of children's eyes, so Jeffrey has transgressed by ignoring the warnings of the police and entering into a forbidden night-side realm in order to investigate the missing ear. Amputation and disfiguration[11].

Both the Sandman and Booth are associated with the realm of nightmare, as Booth repeatedly states in the film: "Now it's dark". During these "dark" moments – i.e prior to raping Dorothy, prior to taking Jeffrey out into the countryside in order to beat him – Frank is at his most powerfully rampant; thus darkness represents strength for Booth. He further identifies with darkness via the disavowal of others' sight, and hate of becoming looked-at, thus as various times within the film he demands that Dorothy and Jeffrey "don't fucking look" at him. This refusal to let Jeffrey look upon him echoes blindness, and of course, castration. It also means that Jeffrey is unable to experience his visual reality but is instead forced into accepting Frank's own version of reality.

"IN DREAMS YOU'RE MINE, ALL THE TIME"

Like a bad dream Frank is only ever seen at night. His only day-time appearance is presented within the context of a flashback. A recollection of the day's events during which time he is only glimpsed momentarily leaving a car. In contrast to Frank's darkness is Sandy's dream that one day all the darkness will be replaced by a "blinding light" as thousands of robins fly free. Jeffrey's journey into Frank's world is framed within the diagesis via the image of the ear – as he enters the grim world so the camera tracks into the damaged and muddy severed ear, suggesting an internal voyage into the psyche, whilst at the film's end the camera tracks back through a clean ear, emerging from its contours to reveal Jeffrey's face as he lies on the grass outside his parent's home. Such a framing device serves to once again identify Frank as belonging to an unconscious/dark/dream-like world, rather than the bright-sunny world of the everyday.

Frank's behaviour is governed by pure desire untainted by morality, the world in which he inhabits is the world of the id – the dark, ungovernable world in which instincts demand gratification. The figure of Booth invades Jeffrey's world. Booth is a nightmare made flesh. He knows that Jeffrey has seen too much – like Nathaniel in *The Sandman* – and must be punished for this transgression.

Frank Booth represents a nightmarish force characterized by his unrestrained and undirected libido, as he states as the gang leave Ben's apartment: "I'll fuck anything that moves". Ben is identified as homosexual via his costume, gestures, and the iconography of his apartment, and – when Ben mimes to Roy Orbison's song, "In Dreams" – Frank looks at Ben with the same intense emotional expression as when he watches Dorothy sing in the night club scenes. Further, as Andy Warhol told his diarist: "Oh, and Dennis told me the other night that they cut the scene out of **Blue Velvet** where he rapes Dean Stockwell or Dean Stockwell rapes him and there is lipstick on somebody's ass"[12].

Throughout the film Booth screams "fuck" at the top of his voice; for example – prior to raping Dorothy – he screams "Baby wanna fuck" repeatedly. Later in the film he demands that Ben drink a toast "to fuck" (note "fuck" i.e. "to fuck" as: concept/as negation/as linguistic outpouring, not to the act of fucking) for Booth fuck is command/statement of fact/and an outpouring of aggression-as-punctuation. In the original shooting script (in a sequence absent from the final British release of the film) when Jeffrey awakens – having been beaten by Frank – his trousers have been taken down, and the phrase "fuck you" is written on his legs in lipstick, once more symbolizing castration and Frank's sexual aggression.

A further link to the dream world which Frank inhabits is provided in Frank's threat to Jeffrey that – should Jeffrey continue to be a friend of Dorothy's – then he will receive "a love letter", which for Frank is a bullet fired from a gun ("I'll take you to Hell, fucker!"). Immediately prior to the film's closing confrontation between Frank and Jeffrey the song "Love Letters", sung by Kitty Lester, features on the non-diagetic soundtrack. The lyrics state that love letters "keep us so near while apart/I'm not alone in the night..." (the lyrics also form a corollary to those of "In Dreams"); Booth is therefore intrinsically familiar to Jeffrey – a fact which Frank recognizes even as Jeffrey attempts to define his morality by defending Dorothy; as Frank states: "You're like me". Booth merely articulates the desires repressed in Jeffrey. Desires which emerge in Jeffrey's dreams during which he re-experiences transmuted forms of the Booth/Vallens relationship.

Booth represents the dark side of the psyche, acting as Jeffrey's darker double. If, as has been suggested by several film critics, MacLachlan may be read as Lynch's cinematic alter ego (in **Dune** [1984], **Blue Velvet** and the television series *Twin Peaks* [1989]), then by creating Booth as Jeffrey's other, with all the attendant acts of doubling, then Booth should similarly be interpreted as the repressed dark-side of Lynch.

*"Knowing this one phone call was crucial, I **became** Frank. I had to cut through the shit and let Lynch know he needed me."*

—Dennis Hopper

Frank Booth emerges in the text as a pure force of nature. He is uncontrolled and his atavistic psyche screams in barely contained ferocity; his every word, gesture and movement betray an imminence of psychosis, as if he is suspended eternally within a moment prior to complete insanity. Dennis Hopper's legendary assertion to David Lynch, upon reading the **Blue Velvet** script, that "I *am* Frank Booth"[13] is therefore a telling comment on the actor's lingering mental state in the early to mid-eighties[14]. Hopper brought such authenticity to the role that it became the signifier of his modern screen persona, to the extent that he has since been condemned to reprise/parody it, to often cartoon extremes, in such films as **Red Rock West, Speed, Waterworld,** and even **Super Mario Bros** (the notable exception being **Paris Trout,** in which Hopper's phenomenal eponymous performance is disturbingly convincing).

David Lynch had already commenced with location photography when Hopper approached him with regards to portraying Booth. Hopper had seen his own dark side, but – by the mid-eighties – had also escaped from it. Frank was one of a trio of roles Hopper played, in his own words, "straight and sober"[15] (the others were: Feck in Tim Hunter's **River's Edge** [1986] and Shooter in David Anspaugh's **Hoosiers** [1986]). Hopper was one of the very few actors who would be able to approach a role such as Frank Booth.

Hopper suggested that Booth was one of the greatest male obsessive romantic leads in cinema, and he was able to offer an interpretation of Lynch's script in which Frank – rather than just being constructed as a purely psychotic criminal figure – was also genuinely in love with Dorothy. Hopper made it clear that Frank was "sick", but suggested that despite his psychosis (which Hopper indicated could be fuelled by the amount of drugs Frank consumes within the narrative) Frank's emotional response and obsession for Dorothy were genuine; "Frank's ablaze with desire for Dorothy. Here's a guy who'll go to any lengths – he kidnaps her, cuts her fucking husband's ear off with a pair of scissors, which isn't an easy thing to do, and ultimately he even shoots the cop he's in cahoots with. Now if that isn't true love what the fuck is?"[16]

Hopper was able to access his own experiences and use them to inform his performance of Frank. He was able to recognize that while Frank represents an aspect of the dark, primitive, and feral side of the subject – the part of the psyche that is repressed in most people – he nevertheless is still human. In articulating this he does not allow Frank to emerge as either a villainous cliché or as "evil", instead Hopper was able to find an empathic

element within his portrayal: "My main concern was to make Frank more... not sympathetic so much, because that would involve in some way patronising the fucker, which would be an insult to him and the audience. But when he's in the club and Dorothy's singing you see him crying, tears rolling down, all over this maudlin old pop tune. That was one of my main contributions. To make him more human, more real. I think there's a little of Frank in every man, don't you?"[17]

Following the years spent on the fringes of the Hollywood industry, Hopper's critically acclaimed performance in **Blue Velvet** was not only one of the best of his career, but also marked his return. In his portrayal of Frank

Booth, Hopper created one of the most memorable screen characters of all time, creating a "psycho" who would in many ways be seen as the benchmark by which others would be judged.

NOTES

1. At one point Lynch considered producing the film in black and white rather than colour.

2. David Lynch cited in Michel Chion, *David Lynch*, BFI Publishing, 1995, p.84.

3. For a thorough psychoanalytic exploration of the film see, for example, Barbara Creed's "A Journey Through Blue Velvet: Film, Fantasy And The Female Spectator", in *New Formations*, no 6, 1988.

4. Whilst as metanarrative psychoanalysis is criss-crossed with fractures and faultlines it nevertheless provides a basis with which to commence a textual exploration of **Blue Velvet**. A text which itself suggests a psychoanalytic interpretation given its central signifier; a dismembered ear crawling with ants, which recalls the iconographic reservoir manifested in-and-across the early, Freudian-influenced Surrealistic paintings of Salvador Dali, as well as specific scenes in the Dali/Luis Bunuel film collaboration **Un Chien Andalou** (1928). Further, David Lynch's fascination with the relationship between dream/hallucinatory state and reality, would also suggest a potential for psychoanalytical textual exploration.

5. See Jean Laplanche and J.B. Pontalis, *The Language Of Psychoanalysis*, Hogarth Press & The Institute of Psychoanalysis, p.332.

6. The older members of the community warn Jeffrey off his quest, not only literally like Detective Williams, but also metaphorically. Jeffrey's mother and aunt warn him not to go to Lincoln when he first goes out with Sandy, immediately afterwards Sandy shows Jeffrey the Deep River apartments where Dorothy lives, as the two return to their neighbourhood the camera – accompanied by generic "sinister" music – sweeps up to a street sign, that reads "Lincoln". Further, the song which unites Jeffrey and Sandy within the film – sung by Julie Cruise in her recognizable high-pitched quasi-child-style – is called "Mysteries Of Love".

7. Sigmund Freud, "The Sexual Life Of Human Beings", *Introductory Lectures On Psychoanalysis*, Penguin Freud Library volume 1, 1991 (1973), p.361. Note also that Freud speculates that the young child may believe that pregnancy could be the result of ingesting "something" – prior to his molestation of Dorothy, Frank inhales gas – the nature of which remains a mystery throughout the film – from a compressed air cylinder. Breathing-in deeply through a mask that fits over his nose and mouth, the sound of his inhalation emphasizes that the fantasy of witnessing parental intercourse can also be triggered by hearing the sounds of parental sexual activity.

8. Sigmund Freud, "The Uncanny", in *Art And Literature*, Penguin Freud Library volume 14, 1990 (1953), p.347.

9. Ibid, p.364.

10. E.T.A Hoffman, *Tales Of Hoffman*, Penguin Books: London, 1982, p.89.

11. Hopper carried this amputation fetish into his next role, as the one-legged, plastic-doll-fucking Feck in **River's Edge**.

12. Andy Warhol, *The Andy Warhol Diaries*, Pat Hackett, ed, Simon And Schuster Ltd: London, 1989, p.784. Sexual ambivalence and homoerotic violence, clandestine night rites, and a metatextual pop soundtrack – specifically in the shared use of Bobby Vinton's "Blue Velvet" – are just three motifs aligning Lynch's film to Kenneth Anger's **Scorpio Rising**; Hopper's role as psycho biker Chino in **The Glory Stompers** perhaps being the "missing link".

13. Lynch reportedly cast Hopper as Frank following a late night telephone conversation: "Dennis Hopper called me up one day, after reading the script. He said, 'David, you have to let me play Frank, because I *am* Frank'. That scared the hell out of me." (David Lynch, quoted in Nick Kent, "The Dark Stuff", *The Face*, no. 88, August 1987.) A similar view of Hopper-as-Frank was reiterated by Jerry Casale, who described the Hopper of the seventies as behaving "like Frank in **Blue Velvet**. It was a put-on but he'd never take it off. ...so Dennis Hopper would turn into Frank and never come off it". (Casale, quoted in V.Vale & Andrea Juno, eds, *ReSearch* no. 11, *Pranks*, ReSearch Publications: San Francisco, 1987, p.197.

14. **Blue Velvet** was shot only two or three years after Hopper's terminal nervous collapse in the Mexican wilderness, which resulted in his successful stint in de-tox.

15. Dennis Hopper, quoted in Nick Kent, "The Dark Stuff", *The Face*, no. 88, August 1987, p.113.

16. Ibid, p.46.

17. Ibid, p.46.

SMALL TOWN APOCALYPSE:
NOTES ON 'RIVER'S EDGE'

"Probably gonna die in this town/Lived here my whole life"
—"Kerosene", Big Black

"You do stuff, and then it's done, and then you die"
—Samson, **River's Edge**

In the 1980s, John Hughes' brat-pack movies were considered to be the dominant form of representation of the "ordinary" lives of American teenagers, and even today they are still considered to be accurate reflections of growing up during the '80s. Through a string of films including **Sixteen Candles** (1984), **The Breakfast Club** (1985), **Weird Science** (1985), **Ferris Bueller's Day Off** (1986), and **She's Having A Baby** (1988), Hughes created an image of the urban American teen as predominately middle-class[1], both loved and loving, and able to overcome the odds in order to achieve their desires. These films painted a picture of America under Reagan that was simultaneously sexy, urban, sophisticated, and upwardly mobile, but they were ultimately a depoliticized fantasy, radically different from the life experiences of many young people.

In 1986 Tim Hunter directed **River's Edge**, a film which was in dramatic contrast to the smothering mindlessness that characterized Hughes' work. Whilst Hughes' films dealt with the cultural mythologies of romance and success as manifest destiny, Neal Jimenez's script for **River's Edge** was rooted in the bleak nihilism of actuality. Jimenez's script was inspired by events surrounding the murder of Marcy Conrad in the small Californian town of Milpitas, which lay to the north of San Jose. In 1981, teenage student Conrad was strangled to death by her overweight boyfriend Jacques Broussard and her body – clad in only a brown tank top bearing the legend "Spoiled Rotten", and white socks – was left near the Calaveras Reservoir. Following the brutal murder Broussard, along with numerous friends, went to view the corpse, drink beer, smoke pot and hang out. Some of the teenagers reportedly dropped stones on Marcy's face. Nobody told the police. When Broussard was eventually tried he received a sentence of twenty-five years to life, whilst others who had visited the body received lesser sentences for their (in)actions.

River's Edge opens at dawn with the moments immediately following the murder of Jamie (Danyi Deats) by her boyfriend Samson (Daniel Roebuck). Twelve-year-old Tim (Joshua John Miller) sees Samson on the river bank and

steals some beer for him in exchange for a lift home. They drive via the home of Feck (Dennis Hopper), a pot-dealing, one-legged ex-biker, who lives as a recluse with an inflatable sex-doll, Ellie, for company. Tim's elder brother, Matt (Keanu Reeves), and his friend Layne (Crispin Glover) drive to school via Feck's house where they too score a joint.

At school Samson tells the assembled group of teens that he has killed Jamie, and takes Matt and Layne to see the corpse. The frenetic Layne immediately understands the gravity of the situation, recognizing that disposing of the corpse and protecting Samson will be a test of the gang's loyalties. That evening Layne brings Clarissa (Ione Skye), Tony (Josh Richman), Maggie (Roxana Zal) and Mike (Phil Brock) to see the corpse. Nobody – including Samson – wants to help dispose of the body. Later that evening Matt decides to call the police. He is taken into custody and questioned; whilst his lack of emotion puzzles the officers, he is soon released. Meanwhile Layne hides Samson at Feck's house, before driving down to the river and pushing the body into the water. It is discovered later by the police a little distance down stream, caught up in riverside fauna.

Layne – now swallowing speed – believes that Mike has informed the police, and begins to drive around town in order to collect enough money from the gang to send Samson to Portland. Following an argument with his

step father and a fight with Tim, Matt walks out of the house, and meeting with Layne he drives to Clarissa's house. Clarissa thinks that Layne is too concerned for John yet does not care for their dead friend, and the two fight. Layne kicks Clarissa from the car telling her to walk home, Matt leaves the car and walks with Clarissa. Meanwhile Feck, who has also murdered a woman, questions Samson on his motives and is shocked by the teenagers' nihilism. Sitting on the riverbank the two argue about their respective crimes, and Samson mocks Feck's love for his sex-doll. Matt and Clarissa spend the night making love in sleeping bags near the river, whilst Tim and a friend break into Feck's house searching for his gun.

At dawn a gun-shot wakes Matt and Clarissa. At a crossroads Layne's VW Beetle idles as he sleeps; he is woken by the police knocking on the car window. Feck walks alone into his home, where he is beaten unconscious by Tim. The police question Layne but release him, arresting Feck shortly afterwards. At school Clarrisa is confronted by her teacher, who demands to know why the students seem so indifferent to Jamie's killing. That afternoon the gang meet down by the river. In the bushes downstream they see the tangled form of Feck's sex-doll. Layne arrives and accuses Mike of being the narc, before attacking him. Matt breaks the fight apart and Layne runs away – hysterically condemning the group for their lack of friendship and loyalty to one another. As Layne runs away he stumbles across Samson's corpse, where it has been left by Feck. As the teenagers run to view the body Tim emerges and points Feck's gun at Matt, planning to execute vengeance for the bullying he has suffered. Following a tense stand-off Matt apologizes and the brothers embrace. Later, from his hospital bed, Feck contrasts his crimes with Samson's murder of Jamie. The teenagers attend Jamie's funeral. End.

Although initially skeptical about directing another movie about teenagers – having previously directed the rights-of-passage drama **Tex** (1982) – Hunter was won over when he saw Jimenez's script, which avoided moralizing in favour of an ambivalence which allowed the characters to respond to events according to their own standards: "I like stories about how people respond to specific events in their lives, which to a large extent are outside their design or control, how they interpret that experience and grow from it, or fail to grow from it"[2]. Hunter was a natural to direct the nihilistic movie, having previously co-scripted **Over The Edge** (Jonathan Kaplan, 1979) with Charles S Haas. Like **River's Edge**, **Over The Edge** depicts a group of rootless teenagers, and – whilst more clearly a fictional film – it nevertheless reveals Hunter's ability to depict alienated youth in a naturalistic style[3].

River's Edge was produced for less than two million dollars by Midge Sanford and Sarah Pillburg, who had also produced **Desperately Seeking Susan** (Susan Seidelman, 1985) and had a track record with low-budget independent films. The money was raised – in part – thanks to the casting of Crispin Glover, who had appeared in Robert Zemeckis' **Back To The Future** (1985) the previous year and was the biggest name attached to the project (whilst Keanu Reeves would soon go on to stardom, in 1986 he was unknown). However, despite the critical acclaim for the film following its premier screening in Seattle, and subsequent festival screenings, the American distributors delayed the release of **River's Edge** for several months, uncertain of how to market such a challenging film.

In **River's Edge** youth is depicted as fluctuating between ennui, abjection, alienation, and nihilism. Isolated from the cities that form the cosmopolitan backdrop to Hughes' narratives, stranded in an unnamed small town located somewhere in the West[4], the nearest the protagonists of **River's Edge** get to an urban centre is to fantasize about moving to Portland.

The bright sunshine, blue skies, and clear air that light Hughes' films (and worldview) are replaced in **River's Edge** by an all-pervasive feeling of dampness, highlighted by the narrative's emphasis on dawn and dusk. The film opens with mist over the river bank, and – despite the glimmer of sunshine during the daytime sequences shot at the school – action is predominantly filmed in shade, such as the leafy pathway to Feck's house, and the river bank below the bridge; even the corpse is located in shrubs. On the occasions that the sky is seen in the film it is predominately bleached white-gray with high cloud.

With the emphasis on shadow and on the greyness of the light, Frederick Elmes' cinematography serves to emphasize the flatness of the protagonists' lives in the small town in which they live[5], suspending them against a background in which they never appear to be fully integrated, thus emphasizing their alienation and distance.

In sharp contrast to John Hughes' work – which is characterized by soundtracks made up from "classic" '80s pop songs and predominantly the dire glut of so-called "New Wave" songs characterized by their appeal to faux-existential-naseua – the diagetic soundtrack to **River's Edge** consists mainly of songs by Slayer, and similar punk-into-metal music by bands such as Hallow's Eve and Agent Orange. Metal is a genre that the protagonists embrace because the songs are characterized by a sense of immediate gratification and power, the music empowers them against the alienation and poverty experienced in their daily lives.

Whilst the characters in Hughes' movies discuss topics such as family lives, parties, dates, school, ambitions, pleasures, and themselves, the characters in **River's Edge** focus on pot, alcohol, and sex, but with a cold distance rather than enthusiasm. Their conversations frequently refer to film and television culture – as if they have no other collective experience or reference point – and even fantasy is articulated via pop-cultural references, including the possibility of stealing their parent's money and hitting the road "like in Easy Rider".

Layne, in many ways the most apparently emotional of the group, articulates the crisis facing them as "like a movie" in which they have to "test our loyalty against all odds". Layne's emotions are simulacra, his conception of loyalty and friendship owing more to media manifestations such as Chuck Norris and *Starsky And Hutch* than any actual social-relationships manifested within the diagesis. While kicking Clarissa from his car, Layne explains that he is helping Samson not because he disliked Jamie but because whilst Jamie is dead, Samson is still alive; but such a statement is irrelevant, appealing to a collective experience of unity that is non-existent among the protagonists. Layne's borderline hysterical, high-octane, performance-of-emotion is largely produced as a reaction to his speed-gobbling lifestyle.

For the group in the film, their cycle of beer/pot/sex exists for nothing other than its own sake; at one point Clarissa comments that sometimes she would rather be dead, until Matt states that if she was dead she could not "get stoned". The most significant event in their youthful lives – the murder of a "friend" by a "friend" – passes over them almost as a matter of course. Whilst Clarissa contemplates calling the police she does not, and Matt – telling her that he informed the police – comments that nobody else bothered to. Yet, during his interrogation at the police station, Matt radiates a spectacular blankness, when he is asked what he felt at the sight of Jamie's naked corpse Matt merely shrugs the question away, saying: "I don't know, do you want me to make something up?"

None of the characters shed any tears for Jamie, dead on the river bank, although Clarissa admits to crying when a character died on a television programme. The teenagers are characterized by a vast vacuum, they lack either the emotional or intellectual resources to confront the results of Samson's actions and thus are unable to respond with anything other than blank listlessness. This void is most clearly manifested within Samson, who is indifferent to disposing of the corpse or making his escape. When Layne suggests that the group share the chore of burying the corpse Samson does not want to, preferring instead to head back into town (presumably in search of more beer). Only during the film's final confrontation on the river bank is there any sign of actual emotion – firstly between Matt and his brother, when Tim finally realizes that he is unable to shoot Matt because of their fraternal relationship, and secondly when Layne – his speed-wracked body pushed to its limit – finds Samson's corpse and finally breaks down sobbing.

According to Tim Hunter, Hopper was the only actor who would play Feck; "Hopper was the only person who felt Feck was romantic, and he could play it that way because Crispin changed the film's complexion"[6]. In casting Dennis Hopper to play Feck, Hunter is able to use the actor as a signifier to previous forms of cinematic rebellion, most clearly Hopper's own **Easy Rider**[7], in many ways the central depiction of the '60s counter-culture. If **Easy Rider** was about the search for an authentic America, a search for love and freedom, and the desire to get high and party, then **River's Edge** is, in part, about the dissolution of any lingering '60s optimism. **River's Edge** is about Reaganomics, and the '80s swing to the political right in American culture. As Tim Hunter has suggested, the teenagers portrayed in the film "see their government more interested in bombs than education, more interested in international debt than in individual communities... There is a sense of hopelessness"[8].

Unlike the rebellious teenagers of previous juvenile delinquency films, the protagonists in **River's Edge** appear to seek nothing but their own psychic annihilation through beer and pot, manifesting a pure nihilism. Political rebellion is no longer presented as a viable option, as the school teacher makes clear; the '60s have "achieved" "great" social changes: "we stopped a war, man," he whines at his class, before telling them that there was a "meaning in the madness". But whilst the '60s was about "meaningful", "authentic", "spiritual" journeys of discovery for youth (classically heading west to San Francisco, or – for the wealthy – trips to

Mexico, India and the Far East), the teens that inhabit **River's Edge** cannot even escape the physical confinement of their own community, with only Layne having a car from the immediate group – although Mike uses his flatbed truck to drive the group to the river in order to see the corpse. They are thus trapped geographically as well as spiritualy and socio-politically.

In many respects Feck can be viewed as acting as an updating of Hopper's character Billy from **Easy Rider**. Feck is an ex-biker, crippled by the loss of his leg in a bike accident, who – having nothing else to do and insisting he is still in hiding for murdering a girl twenty years previously – has stayed in his house for the last five years, dealing pot (described in the film as "Feckweed"), getting high, and dancing with his inflatable sex-doll.

Feck appears as an unstable loser; unable to come to terms with the world around him he has grown withdrawn and paranoid, opening the door while holding a gun, and always after the cry of "the cheque is in the mail". His only stable relationship is with an inflatable doll (although he states within the narrative that he does not believe Ellie to be anything other than a doll); his other relationships all appear to be with the teenagers, who feign real friendship but primarily use him in order to get drugs.

However, as some critics noted, Feck – despite all of his insane rantings, his prior crimes, and his eventual slaying of Samson – emerges as a quasi-moral figure within the narrative. In the absence of parents in the film – who are all presented as ineffectual or absent – Feck and the school teacher represent the only adults who have any interaction with the teenagers beyond reprimanding them. Both Feck and the teacher represent different facets of the '60s revolt. Feck symbolises the outcome of '60s disillusion and dropping out in order to get high and have fun, whilst the teacher represents the political engagement of the counter-culture. Yet neither figure is constructed as the target of blame for the teenagers' behaviour, and Hunter is careful to avoid crass statements which would be too simplistic and too reductive.

In his portrayal of Feck, Hopper makes the old biker appear as an almost tender character, and – during his conversation with Samson – Feck emerges as possibly the only adult who has ever tried to communicate with the boy. Despite Layne's belief in the existence of the united gang there are no genuine relationships amongst the teenagers, and it is left to Feck to offer friendship to Samson; of course such a friendship is inevitably, ultimately doomed.

It is only Feck who is willing to confront Samson about his crime, and it is only Feck who feels it is necessary to understand Samson's behaviour, directly comparing it to his own experience of murder. Feck tells Samson he killed a girl by shooting her in the back of the head. "I loved her," he explains by way of a justification, before asking if Samson loved Jamie. Samson replies, matter-of-factly, "I strangled mine. She was okay." Feck's

crime was a crime of passion, of '60s romanticism driven by some unexplained existential crisis, while in contrast Samson's crime was an irrelevance, an act marked less by supreme passion than by ultimate banality. Samson describes his crime to Feck as an act which made him feel "real. It felt so real. She was dead in front of me and I felt so fucking alive. ...Funny thing is, I'm dead now". Samson is dead not only if he is caught, but dead psychically.

Later, in his hospital bed, Feck talks about shooting Samson (to whom he is speaking is never made clear, it could be psychiatrists, police officers, or just his own, personal tormented demons): "No hope for him, he didn't love her, he didn't feel a thing. I, at least, loved her and cared for her, you understand... I don't like killing people, but sometimes it is necessary. I lost a good friend today, you know?"

River's Edge – whilst only a minor success on its original release – was vastly influential. Its sequence depicting Tim on the bridge watching the river below is echoed in Harmony Korine's low-budget, small town American masterpiece **Gummo** (1997)[9], while the nihilistic teenagers would emerge again in texts such as **The Decline And Fall Of Western Civilization Part 3** (Penelope Spheeris, 1998). Ultimately, **River's Edge** would transform the representation and understanding of teenagers and teenage rebellion in films, removing all false surface gloss and contributing towards a cinematic space in which gritty, atmospheric naturalism would become a signifier of youth, and the false cosmetic world of Hollywood – with simple problems that could be easily resolved – would be viewed as a construction designed for fantasy and entertainment only.

NOTES

1. The exception being the Hughes-scripted **Pretty In Pink** (Howard Deutch, 1986) in which the film's central protagonist, Andie Walsh (Molly Ringwald) is from a working class background. Luckily, though, she has enough drive and ambition to achieve anyway. It is unlikely she will ever end up standing in damp grass looking at the murdered corpse of a friend and feeling nothing.

2. Tim Hunter, cited in Mitch Tochen, "Sneaking Up On Howard Hawks", *Monthly Film Bulletin*, vol 54, number 645, October, 1987, p.296.

3. The teens in **Over The Edge** differ from those in **River's Edge** however; whilst they share a familiar sense of alienation the teens of **Over The Edge** are portrayed far more as victims of a society that constructs them as a social problem and does not account for the possibility of their existence.

4. In refusing to name the community within the diagesis Hunter was able to use the archetype to signify any/all small American towns, thus refusing to comfort the audience with the luxury of knowing the events transpired "elsewhere".

5. It is worth noting that – also in 1986 – Elmes acted as cinematographer on another view of small town USA, David Lynch's **Blue Velvet**.

6. Tim Hunter, quoted in Danny Leigh, "Loon River", *Neon*, August, 1998, p.99.

7. Hopper has also appeared in other notable teen-rebellion movies, including Nicholas Ray's 1955 masterpiece **Rebel Without A Cause** and Francis Ford Coppola's **Rumble Fish** (1983).

8. *Monthly Film Bulletin*, p.296.

9. Like **River's Edge**, **Gummo** explores the American small town as a zone in which the disenfranchised working class live, a zone under-represented within dominant forms of cultural expression. Heavy metal (or other similar examples of immediate gratification music), fucked denim, guns, beer, cars – if they can be afforded – and fucking demarcate the limits of the teenage social space. Similarly, like **River's Edge**, **Gummo** engages with the forms of realism rather than the mythic representations of teenage life presented in dominant modes of cinema.

"YOU GET SOMETHING, YOU GIVE SOMETHING UP": DENNIS HOPPER IN 'PARIS TROUT'

There's an archaic tome[1] which talks of a God who created the earth and everything that dwells upon it (*Genesis* – chapter 1, verse 1). Allegedly, when this God had seen everything he'd made – having already sent man on his way with the knowledge that it was okay to hold dominion over everything (*Genesis* – chapter 1, verse 28) – he gave himself a colossal slap on the back and decided that what he'd accomplished was indeed very good (*Genesis* – chapter 1, verse 31). An optimistic assumption on his part, because somewhere along the line – in the eyes of those who live by said book – said God also created Paris Trout, a man, who while being a true believer, brought a blurring element to the rules as laid down by the celestial big cheese.

Paris Trout is the eponymous protagonist of the 1988 National Book Award[2] winning novel by Peter Dexter[3], and Stephen Gyllenhaal-directed movie (1991)[4].

The setting for **Paris Trout** is Ether County, Georgia, USA; the year 1949, a time when the pace and general attitude of small town populaces in the deep south was far slower, and much simpler. However, springtime was tainted that year – by the outbreak of a rabies epidemic.

Two years previously, Hanna (Barbara Hershey), a shrinking violet and former schoolteacher, had made the misjudgement of her life, and married the pathologically assertive local store owner and money lender, Paris Trout. While cursing the day she made such a decision, being a God-fearing woman she abides by the marital vows – to love, comfort, honour, obey and protect him, and, forsaking all others, to be faithful to him as long as they both shall live – turns the other cheek, and bites the pillow.

A young black girl, Rosie Sayers (Darnita Henry) and her brother Chester (Ronreaco Lee) set about debunking the Chinese whisper that a rabid fox is on the loose, and that one of its victims lies dead and rotting in a nearby shack. They're as carefree as kids can be – but not for long. Rosie is bitten, and, according to Hanna Trout's voice-over, "That was how it started – a little girl named Rosie Sayers and a fox."

When Rosie shows up at Trout's store, Hanna defies her unsympathetic husband and takes her to the town clinic. Having been frightened by the doctor into keeping her mouth shut regarding the fox, Rosie is also escorted home by the police.

In the meantime, Rosie's big brother, Henry Ray (Eric Ware) – who had earlier loan-purchased a car and insurance from Paris – has a run-in with a lumber-truck. His rust-riddled heap all but falls apart on impact. Incensed, Henry dumps the car back with Paris, and declares he won't pay him a penny. Bad move... he's broken his contract.

That evening over dinner with Hanna, Paris reveals his paranoiac obsession with the notion that she's slowly poisoning him – for his money. Very afraid, Hanna tells him she wants to visit her sister. Bad move... because Paris calls upon their marital commitment to each other, angrily declaring, "You ain't got time for visiting Savannah – *you get something you give something up.*"

With violent ex-cop Buster Devonne (Gary Bullock) in tow, Paris pays the Sayers a visit to settle the debt. Henry Ray legs it, leaving his ill-prepared family to face the music – and do they ever. Following a cacophony of cussing and hot flying lead, Rosie and her mama, Mary (Tina Lifford), are left bullet-riddled in a bloody heap.

Following the incident, Paris gets a visit from his hot-shot lawyer Harry Seagraves (Ed Harris). Mary's survived, Rosie's critical, and Paris is in deep. Even deeper when he's informed – the following day – that Rosie has died. In deep, but unperturbed – 'cause he's under the disillusion that his money can buy him his way out of anything; especially seeing as how he didn't kill anyone. "If someone got shot they did it themselves." All he did was what he had a right to do: try and collect a debt.

Paris's unbridled paranoia accelerates and erupts even more violently when he discovers Hanna visited Rosie in the clinic. Whilst attempting to drown her in a bath, he's once again driven to remind her of their contract, "You got an obligation... death do us part, that's the agreement!"

Paris and Devonne are arrested and charged with the murder of Rosie, and the attempted murder of Mary Sayers. Though wracked with doubt regarding his client's innocence – when viewing the carnage at the Sayers' home, he vomits violently – Seagraves prepares Paris's defence.

Continuing her acts of defiance, Hanna attends Rosie's burial. Bad move... because when she returns Paris is waiting, hammer cocked, chamber loaded, and spewing vitriolic fervour... "You're my wife, my stall, my house... Jesus help those who poison my household against me!"

He orders her to fetch him a drink from the store. Through with his ways and ready to walk out of both the store and Paris's life, providence comes up snake eyes for Hanna – in the shape of two customers – and prevents her from doing so. She fetches the bottle of soda. Overwhelmed by his wife's betrayal, the unhinged Paris forces Hanna face-down onto his desk and brutally fucks her with the bottle.

Both over the edge, they make their self-preservation moves. While in her head Hanna has already left Paris, even though she's lost all sense of self-esteem at his hands, she's incapable of breaking the marital/religious ties

that bind them – so she physically locks herself in her bedroom. Paris reacts by transforming his part of the house into a bizarre fortress – a man's home is his castle – completely covering his bedroom floor with glass.

In a further act of torment and an expression of the paranoiac tendency that tells him Hanna's poisoning him – "An ounce of prevention is worth a pound of cure!" – Paris trashes a fridge full of food. Though not wishing to leave the safety of her room, Hanna intervenes to save her only source of sustenance, and suffers a gashed foot. Paris leaves, sated and secure in the knowledge that what he's done is right, that Hanna will understand, and she'll be there when he returns.

Seagraves shows up, but instead of briefing Paris on the following day's trial, he comforts Hanna. Having initially lied to him, she reveals that Paris caused her injury, because he believes she's trying to poison him. Although Seagraves is shocked and clearly attracted to Hanna, he still intimates that she do nothing to harm her husband's case. Then she does leave – and takes up residence at a hotel in town.

As the trial takes place, Seagraves makes two unsurprising confessions to Hanna: that, convinced of Paris's guilt, the only thing preventing him quitting the case is his professional obligation to defend him; and exactly how he feels emotionally towards her. Temptation takes over. They hug, they kiss and they fuck.

While Chester and Mary Sayers' statements have Paris and Devonne nailed beyond all doubt, the trial was always going to be their word against Devonne's lies – "Rosie had a pistol. I didn't have a gun. I own one, but I didn't have one on me that day... it was all of them against Paris, he was real nervous – he said he ain't never known a good family turn on him like that..." – and Paris's truculent, bare-faced insistence that what he did wasn't wrong – "I don't know how it happened... I went on a course of honour. I was cussed at, choked and had a gun aimed at me... I started to shoot, I don't know how many times... I'm in the business of helping people to make a living, I've got nothing against 'em. I didn't wanna kill nobody – but I didn't wanna die... it was defence of my own life..."

While the jury is out, Paris tells Seagraves that he knows about his sexual liaisons with Hanna, but seems content to turn a blind eye to the betrayal as long as Seagraves saves his sorry ass. He can't. Paris gets two years for manslaughter and, unrepentant, vows, "If anyone stole from me tomorrow I'd do the same thing again."

Unfortunately, Seagraves fails to take his words to heart. Money talks – in the form of bribes to local officials – and Paris walks.

When Paris returns home, Hanna and Seagraves are on their way out. This time his threat is clearer – "I oughta shoot you like a common thief!" –

but Seagraves still fails to acknowledge it. Even though she is leaving, Hanna is still too wracked with guilt and failure to completely detach herself from Paris. She still believes herself to be stumbling around in the dark with him, directionless and unsure of her real purpose in life.

The delusional Paris, though tolerated by the townsfolk, never recovers from the scandal. But life goes on – though never indefinitely.

During the town's centennial celebrations, Paris decides to return whence he came – his mother[5]. Armed to the back-teeth, he wheels her living yet lifeless body from the old folk's home to Hanna's hotel room overlooking the parade. Then, in an act that is indicative of him finally forsaking his beliefs, and doing what he deplores more than anything – the breaking of a contract – he puts a gun to his mother's head and declares, "I end all my connections with everything that came before." And shoots her dead.

Providence rolls up snake eyes again for Hanna. Leaving Seagraves at the parade, she goes to her hotel room. On entering she is greeted first by her mother-in-law's corpse, then by the barrel of Paris's gun. Like his mother, Hanna is part and parcel of Paris's past beliefs, and therefore now decreed expendable. Seagraves' entrance curtails the execution, but puts him in the line of fire. He takes three bullets – and dies. As Hanna cradles his head in her arms, Paris – at the end of his tether – says, "You ain't never felt sorry for me." Puts the gun in his mouth, and – BLAM!

At the cemetery, Hanna's voice-over reveals her resignation that, whatever caused their directionless paths to cross, she's never going to be free of Paris – even in death.

While the film was widely acclaimed as being a thought-provoking look at race relations, Paris Trout – the man not the movie – has a much more intricate mindset than that of the stereotypical southern racist living in 1940s America. Though racism's an undeniable part of his character – as it was with the majority of southern Caucasians at the time – the reasons behind Paris's actions lie somewhere much deeper and darker than the colour of another person's skin – in the past, and not his own.

A milestone in his career, Dennis Hopper's lead performance is as unpredictable and terrifying as anything he's done before – or indeed since. Having been repeatedly cast in such roles, Hopper has cornered the market in celluloid psychos. However, with his portrayal of Paris Trout, his character's psychosis differs from the psycho-sexual rage of Frank Booth in David Lynch's **Blue Velvet** (1986), or the fugitive, drug-dealing, twisted celibate romantic girlfriend-killer Feck, in Tim Hunter's **River's Edge** (1986). Paris Trout's psychosis is a manifestation of madness born of tradition – his belief in doing right as it has been written down before him, be it via the Ten

Hopper on the set of **Paris Trout**

Commandments, the Marriage Vows, or plain old-fashioned business etiquette. Paris Trout is the tenacious resident of his own world. A world that only exists inside his head, where good and bad, and right and wrong are rigidly defined lines. If anyone crosses those lines, they had better watch their back.

Tormented by the trials and tribulations he continually faces in pursuit of integrity – the physical manifestation of which can be clearly seen in the expression indelibly engraved into the beaten contours of his face – Paris is a man who's rarely experienced love or happiness. His expression is one of an embittered, cold-hearted scowl. A scowl that grows in intensity and menace when he metes out necessary – self-justified – punishment for crimes against his nature. As he doles out his redemptive reprimands, said expression isn't indicative of, or a depiction of, joy. Paris doesn't actually derive enjoyment from punishing people who flaunt a disregard for his beliefs. To him it's a necessary and unavoidable evil. A case of "this is going to hurt me more than it's going to hurt you". An indication of Paris's reliance on antiquated ways and standards. The point at which he's devoid of any vestige of free-will. All his actions are dictated by his belief in preordained rules. It's a tenacity which knows no bounds, specifically when it comes to contracts. Once a contract is agreed upon, there's no bending the rules, no reneging on the deal – another commandment is set in stone.

Paris's greatest failing is his inability to think for himself. His dependency on the preordained directions of others causes a blurring of said Biblical tenets and business etiquette. He is blinkered, blinded to reason, and strays from the decreed path of righteousness. Several such character-damning instances occur at integral plot moments.

Exodus – chapter 22, verse 25... *If thou lend money to any of my people that is poor by thee, thou shalt not be to him as an usurer, neither shalt thou lay upon him usury.*

By selling the clapped-out car to Henry Ray Sayers, Paris fails to observe the biblical rule which prohibits anyone profiting from the poverty of others.

Exodus – chapter 21, verse 14... *But if a man come presumptuously upon his neighbour, to slay him with guile; thou shall take him from mine altar, that he may die.*

A repeat of Paris's conscious deception when selling Henry Ray the car, but also an incident which can be interpreted as being prophetic – in that the car sale is what triggers off the snowball of scandal effect that ultimately leads to Paris's fatal fall – when he takes his own life.

Exodus – chapter 23, verse 1... *Thou shalt not raise a false report: put not thine hand with the wicked to be an unrighteous witness.*

At the trial, Paris's testimony consists of nothing but falsehood – to cover up his blatant disregard for the biblical commandment that decrees "thou shalt not kill".

Then there's the incident when Paris has cause to violently remind his wife of their marriage vows after she had gone to visit the dying Rosie Sayers against his will, while trying to drown her as punishment. An act which defies both the marriage vows and the biblical commandment "thou shalt not kill" – a commandment which he completely fails to uphold by killing Rosie.

Simple ways lead to difficult situations: emotion-fuelled actions and reactions that confuse their perpetrator, blurring the line between right and wrong. No matter how conclusive the evidence you put before them, they will always be right.

There's one hard and fast rule which Paris Trout always believed to be right. One which ironically defied his frequently misguided ways: "You get something, you give something up." In his case he got revenge and false justice in exchange for his life. Hey, a deal's a deal...

NOTES

1. *The Holy Bible* – King James (Authorised) Version.

2. Awarded annually by the National Book Foundation for the best fiction in the USA.

3. Pete Dexter also wrote the movie's screenplay.

4. While **Paris Trout** was Gyllenhaal's big screen directorial debut – outside of the USA, as its initial domestic exposure was exclusive to the Showtime cable channel via an output deal with Viacom – he had already received an Emmy for **Killing In A Small Town** (1990).

5. In the movie's opening scene, Paris is seen visiting his senile and totally incapacitated mother in a home.

A DENNIS HOPPER FILMOGRAPHY

Rebel Without A Cause (1955)
I Died A Thousand Times (1955)
The Jagged Edge (1955)
Giant (1956)
Gunfight At The O.K. Corral (1957)
The Story Of Mankind (1957)
From Hell To Texas (1958, *aka* The Hell-Bent Kid
      aka **Manhunt**)
The Young Land (1959)
Key Witness (1960)
Night Tide (1961)
The Sons Of Katie Elder (1965)
Queen Of Blood (1966, *aka* Flight To A Far Planet
      aka **The Green Woman** *aka* **Planet Of Blood**
      aka **Planet Of Terror** *aka* **Planet Of Vampires**)
Cool Hand Luke (1967)
The Glory Stompers (1967)
Hang 'Em High (1967)
Panic In The City (1967)
The Trip (1967)
Head (1968)
Easy Rider (+ director, 1969)
True Grit (1969)
The Last Movie (+ director, 1971, *aka* **Chinchero**)
Kid Blue (1973)
James Dean, The First American Teenager (1975)
The Sky Is Falling (aka **Bloodbath**, 1976)
Mad Dog Morgan (1976, *aka* **Mad Dog**)
Tracks (1976)
Der Amerikanische Freund (1977, *aka* **The American Friend**)
Les Apprentis Sorciers (1977)
L'Ordre Et La Sécurité Du Monde (1978)
Apocalypse Now (1979)
Out Of The Blue (+ director, 1980, *aka* **No Looking Back**)
Wild Times (1980)
White Star (1981, *aka* Let It Rock)
King Of The Mountain (1981)
Renacer (1981, *aka* Reborn)

Human Highway (1982)
The Osterman Weekend (1983)
Rumble Fish (1983)
The Inside Man (1984)
My Science Project (1985)
O.C. & Stiggs (1985)
Stark (1985, TV)
Blue Velvet (1986)
Black Widow (1986)
Hoosiers (1986, *aka* **Best Shot**)
Riders Of The Storm (1986, *aka* **The American Way**)
River's Edge (1986)
Stark: Mirror Image (1986, TV)
Texas Chainsaw Massacre 2 (1986)
The Pick-up Artist (1987)
Running Out Of Luck (1987)
Straight To Hell (1987)
Blood Red (1988)
License To Drive (1988)
Backtrack (+ director [credited as Alan Smithee], 1989,
        aka **Catchfire** *aka* **Do It The Hard Way**)
Chattahoochee (1990)
Flashback (1990)
Motion & Emotion (1990)
The Indian Runner (1991)
Eye Of The Storm (1991)
Doublecrossed (1991, TV)
Paris Trout (1991, TV)
Hearts Of Darkness: A Filmmaker's Apocalypse (1991)
SnowwhiteRosered (1991)
Sunset Heat (1991, *aka* **Midnight Heat**)
Superstar: The Life And Times Of Andy Warhol (1991)
Nails (1992, TV)
The Heart Of Justice (1992, TV)
Red Rock West (1992)
True Romance (1993)
Super Mario Bros. (1993)
Boiling Point (1993)
Witch Hunt (1994, TV)
Chasers (+ director, 1994)
Speed (1994)
Waterworld (1995)

Search And Destroy (1995)
Samson And Delilah (1996, TV)
Basquiat (1996, *aka* **Build A Fort, Set It On Fire**)
Marlon Brando: The Wild One (1996, TV)
Carried Away (1996, *aka* **Acts Of Love**)
Cannes Man (1996)
James Dean: A Portrait (1996, TV)
The Last Days Of Frankie The Fly (1996)
The Blackout (1997)
Star Truckers (1997 *aka* **Space Truckers**)
The Good Life (1997)
Happy Birthday Elizabeth: A Celebration Of Life (1997, TV)
Road Ends (1997)
Top Of The World (1997, *aka* **Cold Cash** *aka* **Showdown**)
U2: A Year In Pop (1997, TV)
Meet The Deedles (1998)
Black Dahlia (1998)
Lured Innocence (1998)
Tycus (1998)
Straight Shooter (1999)
EDtv (1999)
Bad City Blues (1999)
Jesus' Son (1999)
Justice (1999)

As director only:

Colors (1988)
The Hot Spot (1990)

INDEX OF FILMS

Page number in bold indicates an illustration

DENNIS HOPPER *Jack Hunter (editor)*
MOVIE TOP TEN

DENNIS HOPPER One of the most talented but controversial actors of recent decades, almost as notorious for his off-screen hell-raising as he is for his roles in such powerful films as his self-directed **The Last Movie**, David Lynch's **Blue Velvet**, and Tim Hunter's **River's Edge**.

Jack Hunter (author of film studies *Inside Teradome* and *Eros In Hell*) has selected his own chronological Top Ten of Dennis Hopper's movies, which are analysed in illustrated, in-depth essays by some of the best cutting-edge film critics of today. The result is both an incisive overview of Dennis Hopper as an actor, and an anthology of films by some of the leading cult directors of recent decades such as Wim Wenders, Tobe Hooper, David Lynch, Tim Hunter, Henry Jaglom, Curtis Harrington, and Hopper himself.

Featured films include: **Night Tide, The Last Movie, Tracks, Speed, The American Friend, Out Of The Blue, Texas Chainsaw Massacre 2, Blue Velvet, Rivers Edge**, and **Paris Trout**.

DENNIS HOPPER
MOVIE TOP TEN

easy rider
blue velvet
the last movie
river's edge
out of the blue
paris trout
tracks
night tide
the american friend
texas chainsaw massacre 2

CINEMA   Trade paperback   1 871592 86 0   192 pages   169mm x 244mm   £12.95

HARVEY KEITEL *Jack Hunter (editor)*
MOVIE TOP TEN

HARVEY KEITEL One of the most versatile and acclaimed actors of recent years, always willing to take on new, challenging roles ranging from the dissolute cop in Abel Ferrara's Bad Lieutenant and trigger-happy robber in Tarantino's **Reservoir Dogs**, to the taciturn settler in Jane Campion's **The Piano**.

Jack Hunter (author of film studies *Inside Teradome* and *Eros In Hell*) has selected his own chronological Top Ten of Harvey Keitel's movies, which are analysed in illustrated, in-depth essays by some of the best cutting-edge film critics of today. The result is both an incisive overview of Harvey Keitel as an actor, and an anthology of films by some of the leading cult directors of recent years, including Quentin Tarantino, Martin Scorsese, Nic Roeg, Abel Ferrara, Spike Lee, James Toback, and Jane Campion.

Featured films include: **Fingers, Mean Streets, Cop Killer, Bad Timing, Bad Lieutenant, Dangerous Game, Reservoir Dogs, The Piano, From Dusk Til Dawn**, and **Clockers**.

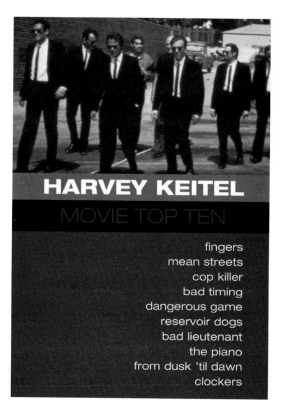

HARVEY KEITEL
MOVIE TOP TEN

fingers
mean streets
cop killer
bad timing
dangerous game
reservoir dogs
bad lieutenant
the piano
from dusk 'til dawn
clockers

CINEMA   Trade paperback   1 871592 87 9   192 pages   169mm x 244mm   £12.95

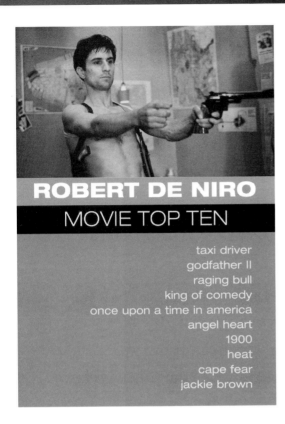

ROBERT DE NIRO

MOVIE TOP TEN

taxi driver
godfather II
raging bull
king of comedy
once upon a time in america
angel heart
1900
heat
cape fear
jackie brown

ROBERT DE NIRO *Jack Hunter (editor)*
MOVIE TOP TEN

ROBERT DE NIRO. One of the most versatile and acclaimed actors of recent years, famous for the uncompromising method approach he brings to roles ranging from the psychotic Travis Bickle in Martin Scorsese's seminal **Taxi Driver**, to the nerveless robber of Michael Mann's **Heat** and the loser in Tarantino's **Jackie Brown**.

Series editor Jack Hunter has selected his own chronological Top Ten of Robert De Niro's movies, which are analysed in illustrated, in-depth essays by some of the best cutting-edge film critics of today.

The result is both an incisive overview of Robert De Niro as an actor, and an anthology of films by some of the leading directors of recent decades such as Martin Scorsese, Michael Mann, Quentin Tarantino, Sergio Leone, Bernardo Bertolucci, and Francis Ford Coppola.

Featured films include: Taxi Driver, Raging Bull, Angel Heart, Once Upon a Time In America, Jackie Brown, King of Comedy, Heat, 1900, Cape Fear, and Godfather II.

CINEMA   Trade paperback   1 871592 88 7   192 pages   169mm x 244mm   £12.95

JOHNNY DEPP

MOVIE TOP TEN

donnie brasco
edward scissorhands
fear and loathing in las vegas
what's eating gilbert grape
nightmare on elm street
platoon
nick of time
ed wood
cry-baby
dead man

JOHNNY DEPP *Jack Hunter (editor)*
MOVIE TOP TEN

JOHNNY DEPP. One of the most enigmatic and uncompromising actors of recent years, famous for a wide variety of movies ranging from Tim Burton's gothic fable **Edward Scissorhands** and lurid pulp movie tribute **Ed Wood**, to Terry Gilliam's psychedelic, paranoiac drug epic **Fear And Loathing**.

Series editor Jack Hunter has selected his own chronological Top Ten of Johnny Depp's movies, which are analysed in illustrated, in-depth essays by some of the best cutting-edge film critics of today. The result is both an incisive overview of Johnny Depp as an actor, and an anthology of films by some of the leading cult directors of recent decades such as Tim Burton, Jim Jarmusch, Terry Gilliam, John Waters, and Wes Craven.

Featured films include: Edward Scissorhands, Donnie Brasco, Ed Wood, Cry-Baby, Fear And Loathing In Las Vegas, What's Eating Gilbert Grape, Nightmare On Elm Street, Platoon, Nick Of Time, and Dead Man.

CINEMA   Trade paperback   1 871592 89 5   192 pages   169mm x 244mm   £12.95

CREATION BOOKS

① KILLING FOR CULTURE
Kerekes & Slater

Killing For Culture is a definitive investigation into the urban myth of the "snuff movie". Includes: FEATURE FILM – from *Peeping Tom* to *Videodrome* and beyond; MONDO FILM – from *Mondo Cane* to present day 'shockumentaries'; DEATH FILM – from *Faces Of Death* to real deaths captured on film such as live-TV suicides, executions, and news footage.

Illustrated by stunning photographs from cinema, documentary and real life, Killing For Culture is a necessary book which examines and questions the human obsession with images of violence, dismemberment and death, and the way our society is coping with an increased profusion of these disturbing yet compelling images from all quarters. Includes filmography and index.

"Well-researched and highly readable, Killing For Culture *is a must-have."*
— FILM THREAT

CINEMA/CULTURE   Trade Paperback   1 871592 20 8   169 x 244mm   288 pages   £14.95

② INSIDE TERADOME
Jack Hunter

Freakshows – human anomalies presented for spectacle – have flourished throughout recorded history. The birth of the movies provided a further outlet for these displays, which in turn led to a peculiar strain of bizarre cinema: Freak Film. Inside Teradome is a comprehensive, fully illustrated guide to the roots and development of this fascinating, often disturbing cinematic genre.

Including: Teratology: freaks in myth and medicine; the history of freakshows, origins of cinema; influence of sideshows on cinema; use of human anomalies in cinema; freaks and geeks; bizarre cinema: mutilation and other fetishes; illustrated filmography; index; over 350 photographs. From the real-life grotesqueries of Tod Browning's *Freaks*, to the modern nightmare vision of *Santa Sangre*, Inside Teradome reveals a twisted thread of voyeuristic sickness running both through cinema and the society it mirrors.

CINEMA/CULTURE   Trade Paperback   1 871592 41 0   169 x 244mm   256 pages   £14.95

③ DEATHTRIPPING
Jack Sargeant

Deathtripping is an illustrated history, account and critique of the "Cinema Of Transgression", providing a long-overdue and comprehensive documentation of this essential modern sub-cultural movement. Including: A brief history of underground/trash cinema: seminal influences including Andy Warhol, Jack Smith, George and Mike Kuchar, John Waters. Interviews with key film-makers, including Richard Kern, Nick Zedd, Cassandra Stark, Beth B, Tommy Turner; plus associates such as Joe Coleman, Lydia Lunch, Lung Leg and David Wojnarowicz. Notes and essays on transgressive cinema, philosophy of transgression; manifestos, screenplays; film index and bibliography.

Heavily illustrated with rare and sometimes disturbing photographs, Deathtripping is a unique guide to a style of film-making whose impact and influence can no longer be ignored.

CINEMA/CULTURE   Trade Paperback   1 871592 29 1   169 x 244mm   256 pages   £14.95

④ FRAGMENTS OF FEAR
Andy Boot

Fragments Of Fear is an illustrated history of an often neglected film genre: the British Horror Movie. The book examines a wide range of British horror films, and the stories behind them, from the early melodramas of Tod Slaughter right through to Hammer and their rivals Tigon and Amicus, plus mavericks like Michael Reeves, sex/horror director Peter Walker and more recent talents such as Clive Barker, director of *Hellraiser*. Films discussed range in scope from the sadism of *Peeping Tom* to the mutant SF of *A Clockwork Orange* and the softcore porn/horror of Jose Larraz' *Vampyres*.

With plentiful illustrations, author Andy Boot unravels a tangled history and discovers many little-known gems amid the more familiar images of Hammer, including a wealth of exploitational cinema, to establish the British horror movie as a genre which can easily stand up to its more lauded American counterpart in the depth and diversity of its scope.

CINEMA   Trade Paperback   1 871592 35 6   169 x 244mm   288 pages   £14.95

CREATION BOOKS

Desperate Visions

THE FILMS OF JOHN WATERS
& THE KUCHAR BROTHERS

⑤ DESPERATE VISIONS
Jack Stevenson

John Waters is the notorious director of *Pink Flamingos, Female Trouble, Desperate Living* and *Hairspray,* amongst other cult movie classics.

Desperate Visions features several in-depth interviews with Waters, as well as with members of his legendary entourage including Divine, Mary Vivian Pearce, Mink Stole and Miss Jean Hill. George & Mike Kuchar are the directors of such low-budget/underground classics as *Sins Of The Fleshapoids* and *Hold Me While I'm Naked.* Their visionary trash aesthetic was a great influence on the young John Waters.

Desperate Visions includes extensive interviews with the Kuchars, as well as a comprehensive assessment of their career and influence. Also included is a unique feature on actress Marion Eaton, star of the gothic porn epic *Thundercrack!*.

With many rare photographs, filmography and index, Desperate Visions is an essential introduction to the wild world of John Waters, and to the outrageous camp/underground film tradition which his movies exemplify.

CINEMA/CULTURE   Trade Paperback   1 871592 34 8   169 x 244mm   256 pages   £14.95

NAKED LENS

BEAT CINEMA

⑥ THE NAKED LENS
Jack Sargeant

The Naked Lens is a vital collection of essays and interviews focusing on the most significant interfaces between the Beat writers, Beat culture and cinema; films by, featuring, or inspired by: WILLIAM S BURROUGHS • ALLEN GINSBERG • JACK KEROUAC • CHARLES BUKOWSKI • BRION GYSIN ANTHONY BALCH • RON RICE JOHN CASSAVETES • ANDY WARHOL • BOB DYLAN • KLAUS MAECK • GUS VAN SANT & *many others*

Including interviews with writers such as Allen Ginsberg, directors such as Robert Frank and actors such as Taylor Mead; plus detailed examination of key Beat texts and cult classics such as *Pull My Daisy, Chappaqua, Towers Open Fire* and *The Flower Thief;* verité and performance films such as *Shadows, Don't Look Back* and *Wholly Communion;* B-movies such as *The Subterraneans, Beat Generation* and Roger Corman's *Bucket Of Blood;* and Hollywood-style adaptations from *Heart Beat* and *Barfly* through to Cronenberg's *Naked Lunch.*

CINEMA/BEAT CULTURE   Trade Paperback   1 871592 67 4   169 x 244mm   288 pages   £12.95

HOUSE of HORROR

The Complete HAMMER FILMS Story

⑦ HOUSE OF HORROR
Jack Hunter

HAMMER FILMS remains one of the most successful and legendary of all British film companies. Their name is synonymous with gothic horror throughout the world.

House Of Horror traces the complete history of Hammer, from its early origins through to its golden era of classic horror movies, and presents a comprehensive overview of Hammer's importance and influence in world cinema.

House Of Horror includes interviews with Hammer stars Christopher Lee and Peter Cushing, detailed analysis of all Hammer's horror and fantasy films and their key directors, and dozens of rare and exciting photographs and posters; plus a fully illustrated A–Z of key Hammer personnel from both sides of the camera, a directory of unfilmed projects, a complete filmography, and full film index.

Third, expanded edition

CINEMA   Trade Paperback   1 871592 19 4   169 x 244mm   224 pages   £12.95

MEAT IS MURDER!

AN ILLUSTRATED GUIDE TO
CANNIBAL CULTURE

⑧ MEAT IS MURDER!
Mikita Brottman

Violent death, murder, mutilation, eating and defaecation, ritualism, bodily extremes; cannibalism combines these crucial themes to represent one of the most symbolically charged narratives in the human psychic repertoire.

As a grotesque figure of power, threat, and atavistic appetites, the cannibal has played a formidable role in the tales told by members of all cultures – whether oral, written, or filmic – and embodies the ultimate extent of transgressive behaviour to which human beings can be driven.

Meat Is Murder! is a unique and explicit exploration of the stories that are told about cannibals, from classical myth to contemporary film and fiction, and features an in-depth illustrated critique of cannibalism as portrayed in the cinema, from mondo and exploitation films to horror movies and arthouse classics. It also details the atrocious crimes of real life cannibals of the modern age, such as Albert Fish, Ed Gein, Jeffrey Dahmer and Andrei Chikatilo.

CINEMA/CULTURE   Trade Paperback   1 871592 90 9   169 x 244mm   208 pages   £14.95

⑨ EROS IN HELL

Jack Hunter

SEX: The history of "pink" movies, from *Daydream* to *Ai No Corrida* and beyond, including the pop avant-garde violence of Koji Wakamatsu films such as *Violated Angels* and *Violent Virgin*. Bondage and S/M from *Moju* to *Captured For Sex* and Kinbiken rope torture.

BLOOD: From *Shogun Assassin* and *Psycho Junkie* to the killing orgies of *Guinea Pig* and *Atrocity*; from the "pink horror" nightmare *Entrails Of A Virgin* to the post-punk yakuza bloodbaths of Kei Fujiwara's *Organ* and Takashi Miike's *Fudoh*.

MADNESS: Homicidal psychosis, hallucination, mutation: *Tetsuo, Death Powder*, the films of Shozin Fukui such as *Pinocchio 964* and *Rubber's Lover*. Post-punk excess, nihilism, violence, suicide: *Labyrinth Of Dreams, Squareworld, Tokyo Crash*.

Eros In Hell examines all these movies and many more besides, is profusely illustrated with rare and unusual photographs, comprising a unique guide to the most prolific, fascinating and controversial underground/alternative cinema in the world.

CINEMA   Trade paperback   1 871592 93 3   169 x 244 mm   256 pages   £14.95

⑩ CHARLIE'S FAMILY

Jim VanBebber

Charles Manson and The Family. The Love and Terror Cult. The Dune Buggy Attack Battalion. Devil's Witches, Devil's Hole. Jim Van Bebber's mind-blowing movie **Charlie's Family** is the most accurate and uncompromising cinematic portrayal of the exterminating angels of Death Valley '69, a psychotic assault of sex, drugs and violence that propels the viewer headlong into the Manson experience.

Charlie's Family reconstructs the cataclysms of creepy-crawl and the Tate/La Bianca murders in vivid relief, showing us not only a devastating acid blood orgy but also the ways in which one man's messianic power held sway over an entire killer korps of sexually submissive yet homicidal believers.

The illustrated screenplay of **Charlie's Family** contains nearly 100 amazing photographs, including 16 in full colour, as well as the complete script and 16 original storyboards. It also includes the definitive illustrated essay on Manson-related movies, written by Jim Morton, main contributor to *Incredibly Strange Films*, as well as an introduction by esteemed underground film critic Jack Sargeant.

CINEMA/TRUE CRIME   Trade paperback   1 871592 94 1   169 x 244 mm   192 pages   £14.95

⑪ RENEGADE SISTERS

Bev Zalcock

From boarding school to women's prison, biker packs to urban vigilantes, rampaging girl gangs have long been a staple feature of exploitation/ independent cinema.

Renegade Sisters examines the whole history of girl gangs on film, focusing on B-classics like Russ Meyer's *Faster, Pussycat! Kill! Kill!*, Herschell Gordon Lewis' *She-Devils On Wheels*, and Jack Hill's *Switchblade Sisters*; Women-In-Prison movies such as Stephanie Rothman's *Terminal Island* and Jack Hill's *Big Doll House*, with Pam Grier; camp SF like *Cat Women Of The Moon* and *Queen Of Outer Space*; plus many other deviant displays of girl power from various genres, right through to Todd Morris and Deborah Twiss' ferocious, post-Tarantino *A Gun For Jennifer*.

Renegade Sisters also looks at Queercore girls; the feminist/lesbian movies of Barbara Hammer, Jennifer Reeder, Anie Stanley and others, and includes interviews with film makers Vivienne Dick and Julie Jenkins, as well as *A Gun For Jennifer* writer/ producer Deborah Twiss. With dozens of photographic illustrations.

CINEMA/WOMEN'S STUDIES   Trade paperback   1 871592 92 5   169 x 244 mm   208 pages   £14.95

⑫ BABYLON BLUE

David Flint

Filmed erotica and adult entertainment has finally come of age. Porn has at last become something that can be increasingly freely and openly enjoyed, and celebrated as a specialist leisure activity in its own right, with its own history and critical lineage. Despite decades of resistance, the long-established hardcore porn production houses have built an alternative film industry, complete with its own visionaries, superstars and standard-bearers.

Babylon Blue examines the '60s roots of global modern-day erotic cinema – from naturist films to the "nudie-cuties" of Russ Meyer – through to various incarnations of Euro-porn and hardcore, charting the rise, decline and resurrection of the genre since the early '70s. Finally, author David Flint expertly chronicles the so-called New Porn Generation – the New Wave of adult movies, as epitomised by the stylish and sophisticated films of Andrew Blake, Michael Ninn and the Dark Brothers.

Visually loaded with profuse and daring illustrations, **Babylon Blue** is the last word on sex cinema, featuring profiles of key directors, producers and performers, and detailed critiques of the finest adult movies of all time.

CINEMA/CULTURE   Trade paperback   1 84068 002 4   256 pages   169 x 244mm   £16.95

13 HOLLYWOOD HEX *Mikita Brottman*

From the myths of old Hollywood to recent on-screen accidents, the motion picture industry has long been associated with violent and untimely death. Hollywood has always been a magnet for suicides, murders, mysterious accidents and brutal mayhem; the simple fact is that, in the age of motion pictures, human death has become an inescapable part of show business. **Hollywood Hex** is a study of films that have, in one way or another, resulted in death and destruction. Some are directly responsible for the accidental deaths of those involved in their creation; others have caused tragedy indirectly by inspiring occult movements, serial killers, copycat crimes, psychotic behavior in audiences, or bizarre and freakish coincidences. These "cursed" films include *The Exorcist, Rosemary's Baby, Twilight Zone – The Movie* and *The Crow*; films that have become notorious and compelling in their new role as inadvertent epitaphs, as documents on the subject of human mortality.

The book contains interviews with sexploitation producer David Friedman, screenwriter Antonio Passolini, director Lindsay Honey and porn actress/producer Jane Hamilton, and includes a stunning eight-page full-colour section.

CINEMA/CULTURE   Trade paperback 1 871592 85 2   256 pages   169 x 244mm   £14.95

DEATH AND DESTINY IN THE DREAM FACTORY
AN ILLUSTRATED HISTORY OF CURSED MOVIES

14 LOST HIGHWAYS *Jack Sargeant & Stephanie Watson*

The road movie: a complex cinematic journey that incorporates mythic themes of questing and searching, the need for being, for love, for a home and for a promise of a different future, and yet also serves as a map of current cultural desires, dreams, and fears.

Lost Highways explores the history of the road movie through a series of detailed essays on key films within the genre. Through these comprehensive and absorbing studies a clear and concise post-modern picture of the road movie emerges, tracing hitherto neglected intersections with other genres such as the western, film noir, horror, and even science fiction.

From *The Wizard Of Oz* to *Crash, Apocalypse Now* to *Vanishing Point, The Wild Bunch* to *Easy Rider*, **Lost Highways** is the definitive illustrated guide to a diverse body of film which holds at its nucleus the quintessential cinematic/cultural interchange of modern times.

Jack Sargeant is an acclaimed underground film critic, and is the author of Deathtripping and Naked Lens.

CINEMA/CULTURE   Trade paperback 1 871592 68 2   256 pages   169mm x 244mm   £14.95

AN ILLUSTRATED HISTORY OF ROAD MOVIES
Jack Sargeant & Stephanie Watson

15 A TASTE OF BLOOD *Christopher Wayne Curry*

The incredibly popular, violent horror films of recent decades, such as *Texas Chainsaw Massacre, Friday The 13th*, and *A Nightmare On Elm Street*, owe much of their existence to the undisputed Godfather of Gore – Herschell Gordon Lewis. In 1963 Lewis, with his monumental splatter movie Blood Feast, single-handedly changed the face of horror cinema forever.

As well as virtually inventing the gore genre, Lewis also produced a number of nudie and roughie movies, as well as sampling the full gamut of exploitation subjects ranging from wife-swapping and ESP to rock'n'roll and LSD. **A Taste Of Blood** details all these, plus gore classics such as *2,000 Maniacs, Gore-Gore Girls, Color Me Blood Red* and *Wizard Of Gore*, placing them in context amid the roots and development of the exploitation film.

A **Taste Of Blood** is a definitive study which not only chronicles Lewis' career as the master of exploitation, but also contains interviews with him and many of his former collaborators, including David F Friedman, Bill Rogers, Daniel Krogh, Mal Arnold and Hedda Lubin. These are interwoven with commentary, extremely rare photographs, ad mats, production stills, posters, and a thorough synopsis of each of Lewis' three dozen influential films. Also included is a stunning 8-page colour section of graphic screen gore.

CINEMA   Trade paperback 1 871592 91 7   256 pages   169mm x 244mm   £16.95

THE FILMS OF
HERSCHELL GORDON LEWIS

NECRONOMICON 1

Andy Black (ed)

Necronomicon Book One continues the singular, thought-provoking exploration of transgressive cinema begun by the much-respected and acclaimed magazine of the same name. The transition to annual book format has allowed for even greater depth and diversity within the journal's trademarks of progressive critique and striking photographic content.

Including: MARCO FERRERI • TEXAS CHAINSAW MASSACRE • BARBARA STEELE • FRIGHTMARE • JEAN ROLLIN • DEEP THROAT • DARIO ARGENTO LAST TANGO IN PARIS • H P LOVECRAFT • WITCHFINDER GENERAL HERSCHELL GORDON LEWIS • EVIL DEAD • ABEL FERRARA *and much more*

CINEMA   Trade Paperback   1 871592 37 2   169 x 244mm   192 pages   £12.95

NECRONOMICON 2

Andy Black (ed)

Book Two of the journal of horror and erotic cinema, continuing the thought-provoking exploration of transgressive film making begun by the first volume. With more illustrated insights into the world of celluloid sex and violence, including:

JESUS FRANCO • SADEAN CINEMA • RUSS MEYER MANSON, POLANSKI, MACBETH • NEW JAPANESE PORNO GEORGE A ROMERO • SS EXPLOITATION • BABA YAGA/CEMETERY MAN WALERIAN BOROWCZYK • DARIO ARGENTO • FEMALE VAMPIRES • SE7EN *and much more*

"Lovingly produced and amply illustrated... engaging... Heady stuff."
—Sight & Sound

CINEMA   Trade paperback   1 871592 38 2   169 x 244mm   192 pages   £12.95

MAIL ORDER FORM   (please photocopy if you do not wish to cut up your book)

TITLE (please tick box)	PRICE(UK)	PRICE(US)	QTY
☐ Dennis Hopper Movie Top 10	£12.95	$17.95	
☐ Harvey Keitel Movie Top 10	£12.95	$17.95	
☐ Robert De Niro Movie Top 10	£12.95	$17.95	
☐ Johnny Depp Movie Top 10	£12.95	$17.95	
☐ Killing for Culture	£14.95	$19.95	
☐ Inside Teradome	£14.95	$19.95	
☐ Deathtripping	£14.95	$19.95	
☐ Fragments of Fear	£14.95	$19.95	
☐ Desperate Visions	£14.95	$19.95	
☐ The Naked Lens	£12.95	$19.95	
☐ House of Horror	£12.95	$19.95	
☐ Meat Is Murder!	£14.95	$19.95	
☐ Eros In Hell	£14.95	$19.95	
☐ Charlie's Family	£14.95	$19.95	
☐ Renegade Sisters	£14.95	$19.95	
☐ Babylon Blue	£16.95	$22.95	
☐ Hollywood Hex	£14.95	$19.95	
☐ A Taste of Blood	£16.95	$22.95	
☐ Lost Highways	£14.95	$19.95	
☐ Necronomicon 1	£12.95	$17.95	
☐ Necronomicon 2	£12.95	$17.95	

SUBTOTAL ....

P&P ....

TOTAL ....

☐ I enclose cheque/money order/cash

☐ I wish to pay by ☐ Visa ☐ Mastercard

Card No:

Expiry Date _____

Signature _____ Date _____

Name_____

Address_____

_____

_____

UK: Add 10% to total price for p&p. EUROPE: Add 15%. Payment with order to: Creation Books, 83 Clerkenwell Road. London EC1R 5AR (£sterling only). US: Add 10% to total price for p&p. REST OF THE WORLD: Add 20%. Payment with order to: Creation Books, PO Box 13512, Berkeley, CA 94712 (US$ only) or order direct from our Website at: www.creationbooks.com

CREATION BOOKS